BRADSHAW'S GUIDES

Volume Nine:
London to Birmingham

John & Jay Christopher

AMBERLEY PUBLISHING

About this book

This book is intended to encourage the reader to explore many aspects of railway travel since Bradshaw's times. Through his account and the supportive images and information, it describes the history of the railways, their engineering works, architecture and some of the many changes that have occurred over the years. Hopefully it will encourage you to delve a little deeper when exploring the history of the railways, but please note that public access and photography is sometimes restricted for reasons of safety and security.

Left: George Bradshaw. Although he died in 1853, the guide books that bore his name continued to be printed and will forever be known as 'Bradshaw's Guides'.

First published 2014

Amberley Publishing
The Hill, Stroud
Gloucestershire, GL5 4EP

www.amberley-books.com

Copyright © John & Jay Christopher, 2014

The right of John and Jay Christopher
to be identified as the Authors of this work
has been asserted in accordance with the
Copyrights, Designs and Patents Act 1988.

ISBN 978 1 4456 4035 8 (PRINT)
978 1 4456 4068 6 (EBOOK)

British Library Cataloguing in Publication Data.
A catalogue record for this book is available from the British Library.

Typeset in 9.5pt on 12pt Celeste.
Typesetting by Amberley Publishing.
Printed in the UK.

On Stephenson's Tracks

This is the ninth volume in this series of books based on *Bradshaw's Descriptive Railway Hand-Book of Great Britain and Ireland,* which was originally published in 1863.

George Bradshaw was born in 1801 and died at the age of fifty-two in 1853. By chance he lived at a time of an unprecedented transport revolution. The railway engineers drove the iron roads, with their cuttings, embankments and tunnels, through a predominantly rural landscape to lay the foundations of the nineteenth-century industrial powerhouse that has shaped the way we live today. It is fair to say that the railways are the Victorians' greatest legacy to the twentieth and twenty-first centuries. They shrank space and time. Before their coming different parts of the country had existed in local time based on the position of the sun, with Bristol, for example, running ten minutes behind London. The railways changed all when they introduced synchronised railway time. The presence of the railways defined the shape and development of many of our towns and cities, they altered the distribution of the population and forever changed the fundamental patterns of our lives. For many millions of Britons the daily business of where they live and work, and travel between the two, is defined by the network of iron rails laid down by the nineteenth-century railway engineers and an anonymous army of railway navvies.

Robert Stephenson, and the statue at Euston, but not the one of his father in the Great Hall.

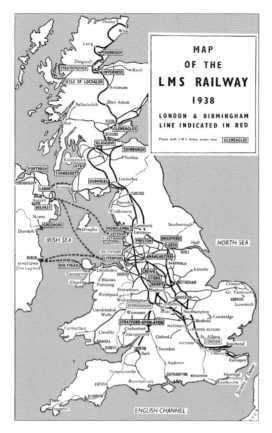

MAP
OF THE
LMS RAILWAY
1938

LONDON & BIRMINGHAM
LINE INDICATED IN RED

Places with L M S Hotels shown thus [GLENEAGLES]

Opened in 1838, the London & Birmingham Railway had only a brief existence as in 1846 it became part of the London & North Western Railway (LNWR). This company in turn was amalgamated within the London Midland & Scottish Railway, otherwise known as the LMS, following the 1923 grouping of Britain's railways. The map, left, shows the extent of the LMS with Stephenson's London–Birmingham route indicated in red.

The timing of the publication of Bradshaw's guidebooks is interesting. This particular account is taken from the 1863 edition of the handbook although, for practical reasons, it must have been written slightly earlier, probably between 1860 and 1862. By this stage the railways had lost their pioneering status, and with the heady days of the railway mania of the 1840s over they were settling into the daily business of transporting people and goods. It was also by this time that rail travel had become sufficiently commonplace to create a market for Bradshaw's guides.

As a young man George Bradshaw had been apprenticed to an engraver in Manchester in 1820, and after a spell in Belfast he returned to Manchester to set up his own business as an engraver and printer specialising principally in maps. In October 1839 he produced the world's first compilation of railway timetables. Entitled *Bradshaw's Railway Time Tables and Assistant to Railway Travelling*, the slender cloth-bound volume sold for sixpence. By 1840 the title had changed to *Bradshaw's Railway Companion* and the price doubled to one shilling. It then evolved into a monthly publication with the price reduced to the original and more affordable sixpence.

Although George Bradshaw died in 1852 the company continued to produce the monthly guides and in 1863 it launched Bradshaw's *Descriptive Railway Hand-Book of Great Britain and Ireland* (which forms the basis of this series of books). It was originally published in four sections as proper guidebooks without any of the timetable information of the monthly publications. Universally referred to as *Bradshaw's Guide,* it is this guidebook that features in Michael Portillo's *Great British Railway Journeys*, and as a result of its exposure to a new audience the book found itself catapulted into the best-seller list almost 150 years after it was originally published.

Without a doubt, the *Bradshaw* guides were invaluable in their time and they provide the modern-day reader with a fascinating insight into the mid-Victorian rail traveller's experience. In 1865 *Punch* had praised Bradshaw's publications, stating that 'seldom has the gigantic intellect of man been employed upon a work of greater utility'. Having said that, the usual facsimile editions available nowadays don't make especially easy reading with their columns of close-set type. There are scarcely any illustrations for a start, and attempts to trace linear journeys from A to B can be difficult. That's where this volume of illustrated *Bradshaw's Guides* comes into its own. It takes the traveller from London's Euston station up the Camden Incline, through Primrose Hill Tunnel and north-westward to Willesden, Harrow, Watford, Berkhampstead, Aylesbury, Bedford, Buckingham, Bicester, Northampton, Rugby, Coventry and final to Birmingham. The asorted branch lines also take in St Albans as well as Leighton Buzzard, Dunstable, Leamington and Warwick. The illustrations showing scenes from Victorian times are juxtaposed with new photographs of many of the locations as they are today, and the accompanying information provides greater background detail on the railways and the places along the route.

George Bradshaw and Robert Stephenson were close contemporaries and were born only two years apart, Bradshaw in 1801 and Stephenson in 1803. There is no evidence that the two men ever met, but they had the good fortune to build their careers as the tendrils of Britain's railway network spread across the map. Robert Stephenson was, of course, the son of George Stephenson and as a young man he had worked under his father on the Stockton & Darlington Railway in the north-east and with him on the Liverpool & Manchester Railway. Although never in robust health, the younger Stephenson had a sharp mind and a thirst for knowledge. The London to Birmingham route grew out of earlier schemes to link the great cities of Liverpool, Birmingham and London. The Bill for the London & Birmingham was passed by Parliament on the second attempt, in 1833 – three years before the one for Brunel's Great Western Railway from London to Bristol. Consequently the L&BR, which opened for through traffic on 17 September 1838, was the first trunk line out of London. The line incorporate a number of outstanding engineering works, not least the many cuttings, bridges, embankments and tunnels – most notably the troublesome Kilsby Tunnel – but lacking Brunel's flair for publicity, Stephenson's most important railway is often overlooked. It does, however, remain a key section of the busy West Coast Main Line route. Robert Stephenson died in 1859, a month after Brunel and six years after Bradshaw.

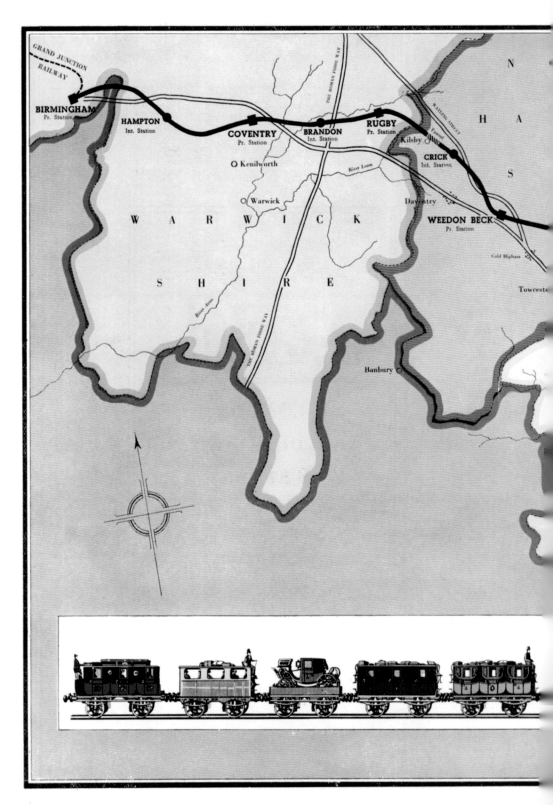

GRAND JUNCTION RAILWAY

BIRMINGHAM
Pr. Station

HAMPTON
Int. Station

COVENTRY
Pr. Station

BRANDON
Int. Station

RUGBY
Pr. Station

Kilsby

CRICK
Int. Station

WEEDON BECK
Pr. Station

O Kenilworth

O Warwick

River Leam

Daventry

Cold Higham

WARWICKSHIRE

River Avon

THE ROMAN FOSSE WAY

Banbury O

Towcester

N

H A

S

WATLING STREET

THE ROMAN FOSSE WAY

6

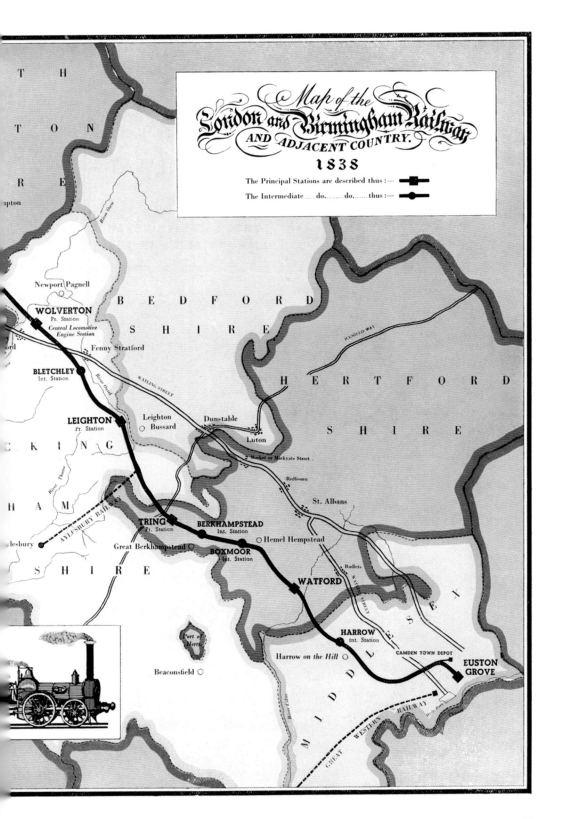

Map of the
London and Birmingham Railway
AND ADJACENT COUNTRY.
1838

The Principal Stations are described thus :—
The Intermediate .... do. .... do. .... thus :—

Newport Pagnell

WOLVERTON
Pr. Station
*Central Locomotive
Engine Station*

Fenny Stratford

BLETCHLEY
Int. Station

LEIGHTON
Pr. Station

Leighton
Bussard

Dunstable

Luton

Market or Markyate Street

Redbourn

St. Albans

TRING
Pr. Station

BERKHAMPSTEAD
Int. Station

Hemel Hempstead

Great Berkhampstead

BOXMOOR
Int. Station

Radlett

WATFORD

HARROW
Int. Station

Harrow on the Hill

CAMDEN TOWN DEPOT

**EUSTON
GROVE**

Beaconsfield

Part of
Herts

BEDFORD
SHIRE

HERTFORD
SHIRE

CKING
HAM
SHIRE

MIDDLESEX

Aylesbury

AYLESBURY RAILWAY

River Ouse

River Ousel

WATLING STREET

River Thame

ICKNIELD WAY

WATLING STREET

GREAT WESTERN RAILWAY

GOODE ENGINE
ON THE
LONDON & BIRMINGHAM RAILWAY.

Left: One of the early locomotives on the London & Birmingham, built by Edward Bury & Co. *Below:* No. 1395, *Archimedes*, of the LNWR's Dreadnought class built at Crewe in 1886. *(LoC) Bottom:* Today's equivalent, the sleek lines of a Virgin Pendolino at the rebuilt Euston. *(JC)*

London

London is the capital of Great Britain, and indeed, if its commercial and political influence be considered, of the civilised world. The British metropolis, if we include its suburban districts, contains the largest mass of human life, arts, science, wealth, power, and architectural splendour that exists, or, in almost all these particulars, that ever has existed in the known annals of mankind. In making this assertion, it should be borne in mind that the power of some ancient cities – even of Rome herself – was relatively, but not positively greater; and that the only well authenticated superiority is that which may be traced to the architecture of a few early cities. The site of our gigantic metropolis is the very best that could have been selected for commercial purposes, as it is enabled, by means of the Thames, to carry on a water communication with every part of the globe. The architectural growth of London, however, may with reason be an object of pride and gratification to its inhabitants. The position of other great cities may indeed exhibit more striking features, but the situation of our metropolis happily combines all which may contribute to its wealth and convenience. Seated on a gentle slope, descending to the margin of a noble river, its plain is bounded on the north and south by two beautiful ranges of hills The growth of London to its present size is most remarkable. In 1560, Finsbury and Holborn, St Giles' and St Martin's, were scattered villages. Westminster was not only a distinct but a distant city. A long dreary road led from Ludgate to the village of Charing – and beyond this all was open field and garden.

We should far exceed our limits were we even briefly to trace the progress by which the City of London extended itself in all directions, and rapidly increased in importance and magnitude to its present position, which is solely attributable to the commercial enterprise of its inhabitants. The annual value of the exports and imports, from and into the port of London, is computed to amount to between, sixty and seventy millions sterling; and articles of domestic or foreign merchandise, including cattle and provisions – sent for the consumption of the inhabitants – amount to the value of £50,000,000, making, with the imports and exports, the sum of £120,000,000 worth of property annually moving to and from London.

The portion of this immense metropolis which is distinguished by the name of 'The City' stands on the north bank of the Thames, from the Tower to the Temple, occupying only that space formerly encompassed by the wall, which in circumference measures about three miles.

When the great fire of 1666 destroyed almost the whole city within the walls, London possessed an architect worthy of raising the fallen capital from her ashes. But the citizens rejected the beautiful plan of Sir Christopher Wren, who proposed to make St Paul's the centre of the metropolis, and to carry spacious streets radiating in direct lines to the principal parts of the suburbs. A terrace was to adorn the banks of the river. The citizens opposed and frustrated this design, and hence the metropolis retains so many of the defects which subject London to the just criticisms of a stranger, on account of all its public buildings being huddled together in nooks and corners.

The Duke of Wellington's home, Apsley House, on Hyde Park Corner with Piccadilly in the distance. Bradshaw describes the house as a 'splendid mansion'.

The daily hustle and bustle in the busy City thoroughfare of Cheapside – the name is derived from the Old English for a market place – which connects at its western extent with Threadneedle Street. Photograph *c.* 1900. *(LoC)*

At the hub of the City the great institutions of the Bank of England, on the left of Threadneedle Street, and the Royal Exchange to the right. Designed by William Tite, the Royal Exchange was opened by Queen Victoria in 1844. *(LoC)*

The first impressions of a visitor to London are generally of an unfavourable character, particularly if he enter it by one of the railway termini, situated in the more thickly populated parts. The dense atmosphere, the squalid appearance of the people, exclude all feelings of pride or admiration from our thoughts. But if he enter London by one of the Great Western roads, from Knightsbridge for instance, he is immediately struck with its surpassing grandeur. On the left there is a view of Kensington Gardens and its beautiful foliage; of Hyde Park, open, elevated, and lined on one side by private houses, some of which appear like palaces. On the right, Belgrave Square, with its magnificence, is invisible, it is true, but the entrance to Hyde Park by three arches, the Duke of Wellington's splendid mansion, and the opening range of buildings of which it is the first, but scarcely the grandest, on one side; on the other the bold and imposing arched gate, surmounted, with the colossal statue of the Great Duke; the Green Park, sloping, open, and ornamented by noble buildings, including the towering structures of Westminster Abbey, Westminster Hall, the Houses of Parliament, and in the distance the Surrey Hills, is sufficient to give an idea of great architectural magnificence, and to excite in the spectator's imagination, some slight idea of the grandeur of London, spreading its great dimensions interminably before and around him.

The stranger who enters London by this road will form a different opinion of it from the one who arrives through a road leading to the city. In either case, however, it must be seen, in detail, to be adequately appreciated.

When we regard the extension of the communications between the metropolis and the most distant parts of the country, and the immense number of strangers who visit London in the course of a year, we believe a short description of what there is to be seen, and how to see it, will not be the least interesting feature of this work.

VISITORS' GUIDE THROUGH LONDON

If the reader be a stranger in London, visiting the great metropolis simply on pleasure, he will most probably wish to walk through the principal streets or thoroughfares first, to make himself acquainted with their peculiar characteristics, as a general basis upon which he may subsequently extend his rambles in different directions, according to the particular objects that attract him most, or the time he intends to remain. Selecting St Paul's as the starting point, the visitor can proceed eastward or westward according to his own predilections. The man of business will probably prefer a visit to the centre of our commercial emporium, the heart of London, and proceeding down Cheapside visit the Exchange and the other public buildings in the city.

The minority of visitors will no doubt prefer going westward first, and therefore we cannot do better than proceed with them in that direction, commencing our inspection of the sights of London by taking an exterior view of St Paul's. For this purpose the visitor should walk entirely round it to observe all the architectural details, and enjoy the feelings of veneration and delight which the striking and impressive view of the cathedral is sure to produce. The extreme beauty and colossal proportions of this mighty temple are worthy of the highest admiration. The front view in particular at Ludgate Hill is very grand. The façade, consisting of a pediment, sustained by a double colonnade, and flanked by two towers, which though not particularly beautiful in themselves,

Above: Sir Christopher Wren, the man responsible for rebuilding the City's churches following the Great Fire of London in 1666, including St Paul's Cathedral.

Left: The statue of Queen Anne in front of St Paul's. Note that the two towers on the west front are different. The one shown here is for the belfry, while the other houses a clock. *(Man Vyi)*

Lower left: Interior of St Paul's three-layered dome. *(Johnny Greig)*

Below: A busy Ludgate Circus at the intersection of Fleet Street and Ludgate Hill, which leads up to St Paul's. *(LoC)*

harmonise well with the rest of the edifice, and give effect to the grandeur of the vast dome which, rising from the centre of the cross, is seen emerging from the two inferior towers, and swelling nobly and grandly high into mid-heaven.

In front of the cathedral formerly stood that famous Paul's Cross, where sermons were preached to the people in the open air, and where politics and religion were mixed up in a manner to which the present times is a stranger. The site is now occupied by a fine statue of Queen Anne. Passing on to the left we enter the cathedral by the door of the northern portico to view the interior, or ascend to the top of the dome and look down on the scene below, at what may be considered the most stupendous and magnificent sight it is possible to imagine. The building is in the form of a cross, having, in its greatest length, a principal nave, divided from two side aisles by rows of massive pillars. Eight immense piers, each of them forty feet at the base, support the great dome of the central area. Over the intersection of the nave and transept swells the noble dome, so much admired from without. It is painted in fresco, with subjects taken from the life of the patron saint, and artists have recently been engaged in restoring those noble paintings, a work of considerable difficulty, when the dizzy height at which their labours must be carried on is taken into consideration.

Around about the aisles and angles of the vast pile are the monuments erected to the memory of the illustrious dead. They are not very fine specimens of art, but we forbear to criticise in the presence of the tombs of Nelson and Wellington, placed in the centre of the mighty temple, with the dome overhead, and all that is grand and imposing around. We can only offer the tribute of our homage of mind and heart to these heroes, whose names loom out from the pages of our history like the giants of a past race, before whom modern heroes dwindle into insignificance.

Pausing for a moment in thought, recalling the simplicity of character, the pure patriotism, genius, and deeds of the heroes whose tombs we contemplate, we could not but associate with their names, that of the great architect, so worthy of being placed on the same tablet with theirs, and then turning to admire the noble simplicity of that inscription over the entrance to the choir, in honour of 'Sir Christopher Wren, builder of this church and city, who lived more than ninety years, not for his own but the public good. Reader if you seek his monument look around you,' and visit Sir J. Soane's museum, in Lincoln's-Inn-Fields, where his watch and other relics may be seen. On ascending to the whispering gallery the visitor can view the concave of the dome and its storied frescoes, then ascend upwards towards the summit, and in so doing admire the construction of the dome, which is really extraordinary. It consists of three separate shells, sprung from a common base, but separating and becoming distinct at the top. The inner one, which forms the dome as seen from within, is of the hemispheric form, it is built of brick. A short distance from its base, is a second dome, likewise of brick, which springs from the first, and ascending with a curve of a much greater circle, goes far above the inner shell, terminating in the key-stone and lantern which support the ball. Still encompassing the second shell is a third, which constitutes the dome as seen from without, and whose curve is thought to be singularly beautiful. It is formed of wood and iron most ingeniously combined, and protected from the weather by a sheeting of lead. It is ribbed and subdivided, not unlike an orange after the first peel is removed.

Left: The iconic image of St Paul's amid the smoke of the Blitz. The cathedral became a symbol of Londoners' determination to withstand their second ordeal by fire.

Left: The wedding cake spire of St Brides, just off Fleet Street. One of Wren's designs. *(JC) Below:* Fleet Street was the centre of the newspaper trade. *(LoC)*

A light gallery encircles the top of the dome, to reach which upwards of 500 stone steps must be ascended, and this is the station from which the most extensive and complete view of London is commanded, affording a glimpse of the most extensive mass of buildings in the world. On all sides, as far as the eye can reach, the solid mass extends itself, along the great avenues, into vast suburbs. The frequent occurrence of reserved squares and patches of green lawns, is the most pleasing feature in the scene. The most conspicuous object, however, is the river, winding its way like a huge artery, beautiful and picturesque bridges spanning the stream, while steamers, wherries, and sailing vessels pass up and down the river. Then the traffic in the streets, the movement along the great thoroughfares of equipages and vehicles, the myriads of human beings hurrying to and fro, is a sight which is quite bewildering and overpowering; so that after extending one's gaze over to the Surrey Hills, and admiring the outline of the Crystal Palace, one is glad to descend and leave the noble temple under the influence of feelings, strangely mingled, of admiration at its grandeur, veneration for the mind which had conceived the idea, the power which had executed this great work, and respect for that religion which could inspire the hearts of men to so stupendous an undertaking. Proceeding on, we descend Ludgate Hill, and in so doing admire the handsome shops and elegant articles exhibited for sale. At the bottom of the Hill we pass the crossing, in Bridge Street, the obelisk of which is erected to the memory of Alderman Waithman, of reform celebrity; the street to the left leads to Blackfriars' Bridge, and Farringdon Street on the right hand, to Holborn and Oxford Street.

Ascending Fleet Street, the great arterial thoroughfare of London towards the west, we pass on the left the office of the inimitable *Punch*, and a few doors beyond, that of *Bradshaw's Guide*, nearly opposite to which is Johnson's Tavern, where the great and learned doctor met his contemporaries, Goldsmith and others.

A short distance further on, we reach Chancery Lane, the well known thoroughfare, of legal repute, to the right. On the left are numerous avenues leading to the Temple, formerly the residences of the 'Knights Templars', and now leased by the common law students. There is in the tranquil retirement of these buildings, and garden facing the river, an appearance of delicious quietness, when contrasted with the noisy region of Fleet Street. Leaving this most interesting neighbourhood, we proceed through Temple Bar, the western boundary of the city, where the heads of criminals were formerly exhibited. Proceeding on the left side, we pass Essex Street, leading to the river, and the church of *St Clement's Danes*, facing which is the office of *The Illustrated London News*, and a few doors beyond is a magnificent building, constituting the establishment of Messrs. Smith and Son, the newspaper and railway advertising agents. Further on we reach the church of *St Mary's*, Strand, a beautiful edifice, possessing architectural features of great merit. We then observe a noble gateway on the left, which is the entrance archway to Somerset House, a magnificent pile of buildings, in the form of a quadrangle, with wings. Entering the court yard we observe Bacon's allegorical sculpture of Father Thames, and the statue of George III. The edifice is now devoted to the business of Government, and consists of the offices for the collection of the Inland Revenue, the Audit, the Duchy of Cornwall, the Admiralty, the General Registrars' etc. Under the open arches, at the principal entrance, are (on the left) the apartments of the Royal Society, and Society of Antiquaries, and on

Above: The bridge out of Charing Cross station stands on the brick footings and piers of I. K. Brunel's Hungerford Suspension Bridge. Originally a pedestrian link to the Hungerford Market, it was converted for the railway in the 1860s, only shortly after Bradshaw's guide was published. *(JC)*

Above: Monet's painting of Waterloo Bridge with the shot-tower on the southern bank of the Thames in the background. *Below:* The view from Westminster Bridge looking towards the Charing Cross railway bridge with the mast-like structure of the Golden Jubilee Footbridges on either side. Of course most of the elements in this photograph can be included in the list of London landmarks Bradshaw didn't get to see – page 28 has more.

the right, those of the London University, and the Government School of Design. King's College adjoins. The Venetian front of Somerset House, towards the river, is of striking magnificence, and its balustraded terrace affords a fine view of the river.

We will now survey Waterloo Bridge, which crosses the Thames in this neighbourhood. It is without exception the noblest work of the kind in Europe. It is a beautiful object, the arches being all of the same height, and the road quite level, which produces a fine effect. From the centre of the bridge there is a finer view of that part of London which lies on the banks of the Thames than, from any other. Looking down the river, and immediately joining the bridge on the left, rises the noble front of Somerset House – the finest object of the kind in London, not excepting the new Houses of Parliament, which appear too low. A little further on, looking like a green *oasis* in the midst of a dark wilderness of warehouses and wharfs lay the pleasant gardens of the Temple. Behind these rise numerous spires, towers, etc. Lower down is Blackfriars Bridge, rising behind which in unrivalled grandeur and beauty is the dome and towers of St Paul's Cathedral, and below this the Monument, the spires of other city churches, etc., receding till they are lost in the mist which always hangs over the city.

Looking up the river there is not much worthy of notice except the view of the Hungerford Bridge, a beautiful suspension bridge, and beyond, Westminster with the two Houses of Parliament, too far to be seen to advantage. We will therefore continue our ramble along the Strand to Charing Cross. The Strand is a fine street running parallel with the river. This part of the town was formerly the favourite abode of our ancient nobility. Their mansions looked towards the Strand, while the space between them and the river was formed into gardens, terraces and steps conducting to the level of the stream, which was at that time the great highway.

At Charing Cross, a great many streets unite and pour their crowds of pedestrians in all directions. Northumberland House, the only noble residence that remains in this *locale*, surmounted by the proud lion which guards the arms of that family, is a conspicuous object at the end of the Strand. The next is the much admired equestrian statue in bronze, of Charles I. In front to the right is Trafalgar Square, in the centre of which is the appropriate column and statue erected in honour of Nelson, and a recently erected statue of the late General Sir Chas. Napier. Behind this is that singularly dull, heavy-looking building, the National Gallery, by the side of which, standing out in beautiful outline, is the celebrated church of *St Martin's-in-the-Fields*, built by Gibbs.

The National Gallery extends along the whole, of the north side of the square. Although this gallery of paintings is inferior to the great continental galleries, still it is a highly valuable collection, and has been enriched by gifts and bequests of works of art of great value. The collection began in 1824 with Mr Angerstein's and others' pictures, to which Mr Turner's munificent bequest was added in 1881, and, together with the Vernon and Sheepshanks' collections, have been since removed to the South Kensington Museum. If, however, our National Gallery is not so rich in pictures as many of the museums of small cities abroad, it must not be concluded that the people of this country do not value and appreciate the fine arts. It is only by accidental visits to the residences of noblemen and gentlemen who possess the greatest treasures of art that we obtain an idea of the almost boundless wealth of the country in this respect. We think it not hazarding too

Left: One of Landseer's famous lions in Trafalgar Square. Although Nelson's Column had been completed in 1843, the lions weren't added until 1867. As for the fountains, so beloved by the otherwise dry New Year's Eve revellers, they were designed by Sir Edwin Lutyens and added in the 1930s. This photograph is from around 1895. *(LoC)*

Above: Looking across the Westminster bridge towards the Parliament buildings, dominated by the clock tower. *(LoC)*

Left: A view along the Embankment. Shown to the right is the original New Scotland Yard, built in the 1890s. Then in 1967 the Met moved to 10 Broadway, the 'new' New Scotland Yard. *(CMcC)*

much to say that there are a greater number of fine pictures in England than in all the other countries of Europe together; and we doubt not that the National Gallery will, as it is in contemplation to remove it from its present site, and to make extensive purchases of valuable works of art, in process of time, through gifts and bequests, exhibit the most splendid collection of pictures that has ever been accumulated in one establishment.

Instead of proceeding westward through Trafalgar: Square, we will turn to the left, through the celebrated avenue of Government Offices, situated on both sides of *Whitehall.*

The first range of buildings of importance on the right is the *Admiralty*; and further on the *Horse Guards*, a fine stone building, surmounted by a small tower and clock. It is easily recognised by the mounted sentinels in the small recesses on the sides. The building opposite, built as a banqueting hall by Inigo Jones as a portion of the then proposed Royal Palace, is now the *Chapel Royal*, fronting which Charles I was executed.

Beyond, on the right is the *Treasury*, with its fine massive exterior, reaching from the Horse Guards to Downing Street. Pacing this on the left is Whitehall Gardens, in one of which mansions resided the late Sir Robert Peel, up to the period of his untimely and lamented death,

Proceeding on through Parliament Street, we come to the street leading to *Westminster Bridge*, and beyond to the open space, known as New Palace Yard, opposite *Westminster Hall*, the *New Houses of Parliament*, and *Westminster Abbey*. The view here is exceedingly grand and imposing. The statue of Canning seems to personify the best attributes of a constitutional minister of a great country.

Westminster Hall. The external appearance of this celebrated edifice is far less noble than is generally anticipated. Nothing, however, can be simpler or grander than the effect of the hall when seen from within. You find yourself in a vast edifice, near three hundred feet in length, having on every side only plain walls of stone, and no column or obstruction of any sort to intercept the view and break the character of simplicity and vastness. High overhead rises a bold and hardy roof, supported by no column, but propped up with inconceivable lightness and grace on a series of wooden groinings, springing from stone mullions on the side walls. This roof is built entirely of chestnut wood, carved all over, put together with the greatest ingenuity, and richly ornamented with the heraldic emblems of Richard II, by whom it was built. It is almost entirely the same as it was when constructed towards the commencement of the fifteenth century, and yet without any impress of decay. In the various specimens of Gothic architecture which are to be seen throughout the Continent, there is nothing which hears any resemblance whatever to this, for its eccentricity, beauty, and lightness, which no one can observe without astonishment and admiration.

The New Houses of Parliament, or the **New Palace of Westminster**, as it is called, is the largest Gothic edifice in the world. It comprises the *Houses of Parliament*, the *Courts of Law*, and *Westminster Hall*, in one edifice. If we proceed to the centre of Westminster Bridge, we shall obtain a fine view of the river frontage, which is divided into five principal compartments, panelled with tracery, and decorated with rows of statues and shields. The terrace is appropriated to the exclusive use of the Speaker and the members of both Houses. When old Westminster Bridge is replaced by the new iron bridge now

Above: The great clock tower is the most recognisable symbol of the new Houses of Parliament, which were designed in the perpendicular Gothic style by architect Sir Charles Barry. In fact the 316-foot tower is just slightly shorter than the Victoria Tower. Universally referred to as Big Ben, even though that is actually a bell, it was renamed the Queen Elizabeth Tower to mark the Diamond Jubilee in 2012. *Below:* The sumptuous interior furnished by Augustus Pugin. *(LoC)*

in course of construction, the view of the Houses of Parliament will be much finer, as the old bridge is too lofty, and seems to crush the delicate Gothic style of the beautiful building. At present it is seen to the best advantage from the opposite bank of the Thames, along the walk in front of Lambeth Palace, the residence of the Archbishop of Canterbury. The small towers give a picturesque effect to the river front, but the three principal ones, the Victoria, Central, and Clock, do not add to the beauty of the building.

Retracing our steps to New Palace Yard, we enter the Palace through Victoria Tower, a truly royal entrance.

The rebuilding of the Houses of Parliament is the most important architectural work which has been undertaken in this country since the re-edification of St Paul's Cathedral; and it may be added, that in arrangement, detail, warming, and ventilation combined, so perfect a structure was never before planned. The exterior of the House of Lords presents no enriched architectural features, but the interior is, without doubt, the finest specimen of Gothic civil architecture in Europe, its proportions, arrangement, and decorations being perfect, and worthy of the great nation at whose cost it has been erected.

Entering the house from the Peers' Lobby, the effect is magnificent in the extreme. The length and loftiness of the apartment, its finely proportioned windows, with the gilded and canopied niches between them, the Royal throne, glowing with gold and colours, the richly-carved panelling which line the walls, with its gilded emblazoned cove, and the balcony of brass, of light and elegant design, rising from the canopy; the roof, most elaborately painted; its massy beams and sculptured ornaments, and pendants richly gilded; all unite in forming a scene of royal magnificence, as brilliant as it is unequalled.

The House of Commons is in a direct line with the House of Lords, at the north end of the structure, The aspect of the house altogether, is that of plain and business-like serenity, adapted to the deliberation of legislators. The Speaker's chair is placed in such a position that, supposing all the doors open between them, the Chancellor on the woolsack and the Speaker in the chair would exactly face each other. Yet although this palace of the parliament cannot for centuries rival in its associations the humble structure of St Stephen's Chapel, let us hope that the future representatives of Great Britain will not prove Inferior to their predecessors in genius and patriotism.

Westminster Abbey – this noble pile, in magnificence of extent, grandeur of proportions, and elaborate beauty of construction, can most favourably be compared with the noblest specimens of Gothic architecture in Europe. It possesses a symmetrical and homogeneous character throughout. There appears one defect in the external appearance which is sufficiently obvious, and that is, the too great length compared with the height, though this, within, adds vastly to the character of, grandeur and continuity, as you glance along the naves from extremity to extremity. If, however, there are any impressions on the mind at variance with unqualified admiration in contemplating this grand structure without, those impressions vanish as the visitor enters the cloister, and, passing the noble portal, stands in the midst of columns, arches, and swelling naves, surrounded by the mighty dead of England, treasured remains, sculptured effigies, and

Above: Oxford Circus and Regent Street. Bradshaw writes of, 'the noble avenue of Regent Street, the princely edifices of the nobility, many of them built in a grand and chaste style of architecture, and the magnificent Club Houses, render this one of the finest quarters of London'. *(CMcC)*

Left and above: Piccadilly Circus and the statue of Anteros, the Greek god of love who is widely known as Eros. Cast in aluminium, Alfred Gilbert's sculpture of a naked male figure ruffled Victorian sensibilities when erected in 1893. It is, therefore, one of the many post-Bradshaw landmarks of London. See page 28 for more examples.
(LoC/Man Vyi)

recorded epitaphs of those who hive emblazoned our history with, the brightness of their deeds, immortalised our language, and shed undying glory on our race. No one can wander through these precincts, the aisles of the Abbey, examine the monuments and read the inscriptions, without a feeling of awe and admiration, and offering the homage of his mind at the throne of departed genius.

In the chapel of Henry VII the mind is awed by the gorgeous character of the architecture, and the splendour of the monuments which entomb the buried majesty of England's Kings; while above are seen the swords, helmets, and waving banners of the Knights of some of the noblest orders of Christendom, to complete the impression of the scene, and fill the imagination with images of magnificence and pomp.

It is in the Poets' Corner, however, that the pilgrim's footsteps most fondly linger. It Is there that his eyes trace and retrace names, and study lineaments, connected with his sublimest and tenderest associations. No place in the world is so capable of recalling to 'memory's light' so many associations connected with whatever is most god-like in human genius. Supposing each country to have – but alas it has not! – a like hallowed receptacle for the remains of its most honoured children, which is there of modem times that can boast such a name as Shakespeare? Where shall we look for the counterpart of the divine Milton? Where else for the genius which characterised Newton?

The monuments of the Poets' Corner are blackened by time, but the memory of those to whom they are sacred is still, and will ever be, green in the hearts of their countrymen and their descendants, and in every region of the world inhabited by those who speak the language in which they wrote.

That venerable Shrine where repose the ashes of our patriots, poets, and sages.

Upon leaving the Abbey, we will proceed through St James's Park, which we can glance at in passing, to the Duke of York's Monument, at the bottom of Regent Street, and conclude our walk by a view of Carlton Gardens, Pall Mall, etc. The view from the statue over the park is exceedingly fine, embracing the towers of the Abbey and the new Houses of Parliament. On the other hand, the wide and noble avenue of Regent Street, the princely edifices of the nobility, many of them built in a grand and chaste style of architecture, and the magnificent Club Houses, render this one of the finest quarters in London.

Starting from this point the ensuing day, the visitor should wend his way up Regent Street, the first point of interest in which is where it opens into a circus, at the intersection of Piccadilly, leading to Hyde Park, Chelsea, Hammersmith, etc. – one of the greatest thoroughfares in London, or perhaps in the world. Continuing his walk up this fine street, the visitor cannot fail to admire it. The rows of symmetrical and ornamented edifices produce a fine effect – on each side are a collection of brilliant shops, filled with most costly articles, attesting at once the wealth, luxury, refinement of the land, and the acme of excellence to which the manufactures of this country have attained.

Proceeding on, we reach the intersection of Oxford Street, where Regent Street again opens out and forms a circus. This is another thoroughfare between the east and the west, the left leading to Oxford Street, Hyde Park, etc. – the right to Holborn

Contrasting retail experiences in London. *Above:* 'Town Life' in Bond Street, postcard *c.* 1905, and flower sellers at Covent Garden. *(CMcC/LoC) Below:* Another old postcard, this time showing Covent Garden when it was the capital's main fruit and vegetable market. *(CMcC)*

and the City. Continuing our walk along Oxford Street we find the shops assume a still more elegant and fashionable appearance – their extent, neatness, and elegance of arrangement are admirable. Oxford Street consists of a straight line of shops, not less than two miles in length, with a broad footpath on each side, and a carriage-road in the centre. This street is perpetually thronged with splendid equipages, on account of its being the grand avenue in which ran most of the side streets leading to the squares, etc., where the nobility and people of fashion reside. This is called the neighbourhood of the squares, and is deservedly the boast of London. In the whole of that part of the town, north of Oxford Street, there are scarcely any shops, most of the houses being occupied by persons of distinction. This is considered by far the finest part of London,

From Regent Circus, Oxford Street, the visitor may proceed Northwards, passing *All Soul's Church*, with its quaint steeple, and up that street of palaces, Portland Place, to Regent's Park, and the Zoological Gardens.

The Zoological Gardens in Regent's Park, in the season, is perhaps the most fashionable resort of the metropolis. This is an institution which had its origin in that spirit of association which has achieved so much for England. The payment of a trifling subscription, by many people, has led to the creation of a beautiful garden, of a tasteful and pleasing arrangement. Specimens of rare, curious, and beautiful animals have been collected from every corner of the globe; and the study of the structure, character, and habits of what is most interesting in the works of the Creator is thus rendered easy and entertaining to the young. The arrangement of the Species is made with great care and order, and many of the animals are lodged in rustic cottages, in the style of the country from which they come. Here, too, are strange exotic plants – so that a walk through this garden is in a measure like a rapid journey over the world.

Returning from Regent's Park to the end of Oxford Street, the visitor can then enter Hyde Park, and walk through it to Kensington Gardens which is also a beautiful place. Thence retracing his steps towards Hyde Park Corner, his attention will be attracted to the statue of Achilles in the Park, and the colossal equestrian statue upon the top of the Triumphal Arch on Constitution Hill; both erected in honour of the late Duke of Wellington. Apsley House, the residence of the late and present Duke, at the corner of Hyde Park, is also an object of general interest.

Proceeding up Piccadilly the visitor should not omit to walk up Bond Street, to take a view of this the most fashionable promenade of London, where the young men of family take their walks, and exhibit the latest fashions of the day. The shops here are not so ostentatious as those in the more general thoroughfares, but they are extremely elegant, and their articles most recherche, and here the ladies of aristocracy and wealth may be seen alighting from their carriages and splendid equipages to make some purchase, or examine the latest, *modes* from Paris.

Retracing his steps to Piccadilly, the visitor should not omit to visit the Burlington Arcade, the prettiest gallery in London. It is a facsimile of a portion of the Palais Royal, but the tradesmen who occupy these shops are of a less wealthy class, and the place is considered as the fashionable gentleman's lounge.

From Piccadilly the visitor should return towards the city through Leicester Square and Covent Garden Market. In the former, on the south side, is the Alhambra, formerly

Above: Exterior and interior of St Mary-le-Bow. The church was completely gutted during the Blitz and has been extensively restored. *(JC) Below:* Looking across London Bridge with the tower of St Magnus-the-Martyr, and the Monument marking the spot where the Great Fire started. *(LoC)*

the Panopticon. Covent Garden Market is celebrated for being the mart for the most delicate and choicest fruit grown or imported into England.

From Covent Garden the visitor should take one of the streets leading to the Strand, whence he can easily regain his hotel; and the next day, starting again from St Paul's, go eastward, and extend his visit to the City, and entering Cheapside from St Paul's Churchyard, the first objects which attract our attention are the statue of Sir Robert Peel, and the *General Post Office*, in St Martin's-le-Grand. On the right, at no great distance, stands the celebrated Church of *St Mary-le-Bow*, which is esteemed to be situated in the heart of the City of London, and all persons born within the sound of its bells are vulgarly designated 'Cocknies'. The crowd of persons in Cheapside from morning till night is always very great, and prevents any one loitering to indulge in observation or remark. At the end of King Street, which runs northward from Cheapside, is *Guildhall*, the Civic Palace, where the principal business of the corporation is conducted and the magnificent civic banquets given. The hall contains some fine monuments, the two colossal figures of Gog and Magog; and a noble statue to the Great Duke, just completed. Returning to Cheapside, the next building worthy of notice is the *Mansion House*, the official residence of the Lord Mayor. The *Egyptian Hall* is a lofty room of considerable splendour. Near it is seen the Church of *St Stephen's*, Walbrook, said to be the masterpiece of Sir Christopher Wren. The Bank of England is nearly opposite, the statue of the Duke of Wellington in front, and behind this the *New Royal Exchange*. The building of the Bank of England offers no feature worthy of notice, but the interior can only be visited by an order of one of the Governors. It is well worth a visit. The statue of the Great Duke is by Chantrey, and is indeed a noble ornament to the city. The Royal Exchange is a splendid piece of architecture, and should be examined in detail, to see how admirably it has been adapted to the purpose for which it is designed.

Cornhill on the right is as glittering as ever with jewellers' shops, beyond which is Leadenhall Street. Beyond this there is nothing of interest to the visitor, who is recommended to retrace his steps to the side of the Wellington statue, and proceeding thence down King William Street, glance at the statue of the Sailor King, to the left of which is the Monument, and then walk on to London Bridge, the traffic over which, and the view of the river below, will afford him subjects of interesting contemplation respecting this metropolis of a country which, though inconsiderable in extent, with a climate healthful indeed, yet unsuited to rich productions, and on the whole unpropitious, its coasts destitute of natural harbours, and exposed to the inconvenience of frightful storms, has yet risen by commerce to an eminence of wealth, power, and consideration, of which the world has hitherto known no example.

Returning towards King William's statue, the visitor should cross over and proceed down Little East Cheap, and Great Tower Street, in which are the offices of the wealthy city of London Wine Brokers, which will lead him by a short route to that most interesting spot called Tower Hill, and in sight of the Tower of London, which he will undoubtedly visit.

The Tower of London, erected by William the Conqueror, connects itself with every succeeding event in the history of our race. In more barbarous times than those in which we live, it has been the prison-house, and the place of execution of illustrious victims

Above: What would Bradshaw have made of today's living statues and celebrity lookalikes that populate the tourist spots? Jack Sparrow on the South Bank.

The sights of London that Bradshaw wouldn't have seen

The capital's popular landmarks seem so familiar to us that it is easy to forget that many are fairly recent additions on the scene. As Bradshaw reveals, the Houses of Parliament were brand new when the guide was published in 1863, but on the other hand, the Albert Hall didn't open until 1871 while Tower Bridge wouldn't be completed for a further twenty-three years after that (1894). One of the greatest icons of the twentieth century, the red Routemaster bus, first entered service in 1956, ninety-three years after the guide appeared, and its successor, the New Routemaster, followed in 2013, a full 150 years after the guide was published.

of tyranny. Perhaps there is no single spot in Europe, or in the world, so calculated to awaken impressive and profitable recollections, and so pregnant with interest to Englishmen, as this place. Within these venerable vaults, human nature has been exhibited in all its extremes. The pomp of royalty, wretchedness of solitude, horrors of murder and martyrdom, all stand associated with the eventful history of the building. The Yeomen of the Guard, better known as beefeaters, in the picturesque costume of the days of Elizabeth, conduct the visitors, over it. Within the courtyard, a number of objects are pointed out that are rich in historical interest, of the most romantic and mournful character. There stands the Bloody Tower in which the unfortunate young prince, Edward V and his brother, are said to have been smothered by order of Richard III. The Beauchamp Tower is also shown, as the prison in which the ill-fated Anne Boleyn, and the highly gifted and unfortunate Lady Jane Grey were confined, and the small room in which the gifted Sir Walter Raleigh, wrote his History of the World, and which he occupied fifteen years. The Armoury is one of the most extensive in the world. There is one immense room containing, it is said, two hundred thousand muskets, tastefully and beautifully arranged. On all sides are trophies of victories by land and sea, and in a noble gallery called the Horse Armoury, are arranged in complete panoply, mounted, with lance in hand the effigies of many of England's greatest monarch warriors, clad in the very armour which they had worn; and among the weapons possessing historical interest, which are here preserved, is the identical axe which severed the head of Anne Boleyn. The regalia of England is preserved in a very massive strong tower, without windows, and quite dark from without, being lit by a powerful lamp, which exhibits the brilliancy and value of the precious stones. Everything is admirably arranged for exhibition; the imperial crown, and other most precious articles are turned round, so as to be seen, on all sides, by means of ingenious machinery, touched by the ancient dame who exhibits them.

On quitting the Tower, the visitor can proceed to inspect some of the magnificent docks and warehouses further down the river – which are of surpassing importance to the Port of London, and the great commercial interests of the Kingdom, all of which cannot fail to prove of interest to the observant and inquiring traveller.

The Tower, built by the Normans not to protect but to suppress the 'brutal populace'.

Left: Designed by Philip Hardwick, the Euston arch stood 70 feet high. The two-storey station building can be seen beyond the arch on the right-hand side. Both the arch and Euston's Great Hall were demolished in the 1960s as part of the major rebuilding scheme. The new station has been described as a cross between an airport terminal and a bus station.

Above: Interior of the Great Hall with the statue of George Stephenson. The Hall has gone but the statue is now at the NRM in York. *Left:* The only survivors from the old station are the two Portland stone gate lodges on the entrance from the Euston Road. Note the LNWR monogram beneath the pediment and the names of the major destinations served by the railway carved into the stone.

London to Birmingham

LONDON & NORTH WESTERN RAILWAY

EUSTON SQUARE STATION

Passing under the magnificent Doric entrance, which forms so grand a feature of the metropolitan terminus of this line of railway, the huge pile of building at once arrests the eye. It was designed by Philip Hardwick, Esq., and erected by Messrs. William Cubitt and Co., at a cost of about £150,000.

The structure, of the interior, is of plain Roman style of architecture, and is 220 feet long by 168 feet in width. At the southern front there are five entrances. The outer doors lead into what is called the 'outer vestibule', having a beautifully designed mosaic pavement, constructed of patent metallic lead, within a border of Craigleith stone. On the northern side of the 'outer vestibule' are five other entrances, leading into the grand hall or vestibule; and this hall for size and grandeur is probably unique; in dimensions it is truly gigantic, being 125 feet in length, 61 feet in width, and 60 feet in height. At the northern end is a noble flight of steps, leading to a vestibule, in which are doors entering into the general meeting room, the board room, and the conference room, and the gallery which runs round the hall, thus giving facility of communication to an infinity of offices connected with the railway traffic. The style of architecture is Roman Ionic, and has been treated with great skill. The bas-reliefs which adorn the panels in the corners of the hall are eight in number, and typify the chief cities and boroughs with which the North Western Railway communicates. They are London, Liverpool, Manchester, Birmingham, Carlisle, Chester, Lancaster, and Northampton. London is typified by a female figure, crowned, bearing in her hands the sceptre of royalty, and the rudder, emblem of maritime power. Below her sits an old man with a long beard, symbolical of Father Thames, and by her knees a genius, his arm resting on a globe, and at his feet emblems of music, painting, and the drama, indicating the universality of the art of knowledge of the great metropolis of the world. The background is filled with St Paul's and a group of shipping. Liverpool is a sitting female figure, resting on a rudder, with a genius by her side holding a quadrant. An aged man, having shells and corals in his hair, symbolises the Mersey: in his right hand he holds a trident, and his left rests upon a well filled cornucopia. A portion of the Exchange and a group of shipping fills up this characteristic group. Manchester is individualised by a laurel-crowned female, sitting and holding a distaff, her hand resting on a bale of cotton; a genius by her side holding the shuttle, indicative of the cotton-spinning notoriety of the important city. Mercury, emblem of commerce, sits in the foreground, busy drawing plans on a piece of paper, and the background is composed of piles of cotton goods, a huge factory, and the tower of the cathedral. Birmingham has the symbols of the iron trade – Vulcan, with his hammer and anvil being in the foreground; a beautiful vase, showing the variety and perfection of the iron works, and the portico of the new Town Hall, fill up

Above: When Euston station opened in 1838, the departure and arrivals platforms were each served by two lines of track. Note that most of the carriages are open topped, and also the lack of any locomotives. The trains were hauled up the Camden Incline by a system of continuous ropes pulled by stationary steam-powered engines at the top. Downward trains were controlled by 'brake-riders' who rode on the carriages to operate the brakes. *Below left:* A wartime spotter scans the sky for enemy aircraft as the LMS Princess Royal Class *Queen Maude* and an unidentified streamliner pull out of the station. *Below right:* The chimneys of the engine houses at Camden.

the group. Chester with its far-famed dairy produce, its cheeses, its walls, and venerable cathedral is well characterised. Carlisle shows cattle market, manufacture, and maritime symbols, with its cathedral tower; Lancaster its furniture and other manufactures; and Northampton has its emblems, the shoemaker, as well as agricultural symbols, and a home to typify its celebrated horse fair.

The large group in alto-relievo over the door leading to the general meeting room, is an extremely picturesque and effective composition – representing Britannia, supported by Science and Industry.

The statue of the late George Stephenson, who effected more than any other engineer has done towards the development of the railway system, is a very appropriate ornament to the great hall. The statue, which is of fine Carrara marble, is ten feet in height. The figure is habited in the costume of the times, and holds in the right hand a scroll, upon which is inscribed the elevation of an aqueduct.

Leading from the grand hall on the basement, on the eastern and western sides are several glass doors, connecting it with the booking offices and platforms.

London to Cheddington

Upon starting from the Euston Square station the train proceeds somewhat leisurely as far as Camden Town station, passing under arches, and between brick walls, above which may be seen at intervals, elegant villas and rows of houses, the inhabitants of which must be great admirers of the locomotive, with its shrieking whistle, to choose their residence in the immediate vicinity of this terminus.

The train runs up an incline to

CAMDEN ROAD
Telegraph station at Camden. Money Order Office, 89 High Street.

This station is the London depot of the company, and from thence two lines diverge to the right and left, the former going to Islington, Bow, Stratford, or Fenchurch Street, and the latter to Kew, Richmond, Windsor, etc.

On quitting the Camden station, we leave Regent's Park and Hampstead on the left, and the beautiful grounds of Highgate on the right; thence we proceed past Chalk Farm, a spot once celebrated as the scene of repeated duels. Passing on, we enter the Primrose Hill tunnel – thence we are conveyed under the Edgeware Road, and beneath a number of bridges, chiefly used for connecting private property severed by the line. Beyond this is the pretty village of Kilburn and the open country, which now begins to appear on either hand, is sufficiently beautiful to interest the traveller. On the right is the spire of Hampstead church – to the left that of Notting Hill, and we have scarcely time to admire their architecture before we are enclosed in the banks of a deep cutting, through which we proceed a few seconds, and then enter another tunnel, called the Kensal Green Tunnel, the celebrated cemetery – the Pere la Chaise of London – being on the left side, which is worthy of a visit, from the number of eminent individuals who are entombed within its limits. The tomb of His Royal Highness the late Duke of Sussex, the Princess Sophia, Ducrow, and George Robins (the princes of horsemanship and auctioneering),

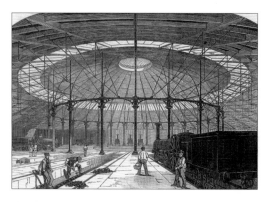

Because of the hill up from Euston, the level ground at Camden was selected as the site for the main goods station at the London end of the L&BR and later the LNWR and LMS.

Above: Two views of the great circular engine shed at Camden, now a concert venue known as the Roundhouse. Completed in 1847, with a diameter of 160 feet it could accommodate up to twenty-four locos around a central turntable.

Left: 1935 poster by Norman Wilkinson showing several scarlet LMS locos in front of Camden Engine Shed. Many of the railway buildings and warehouses have survived and have been absorbed within Camden's famous market area.

Lower left: From *The LMS at War*, an illustration of one of the frequent air raids on the marshalling yards at Willesden in September 1940.

are worth a visit. The cemetery approaches the railway, and extends over a part of the tunnel. The railway now enters a richly pastoral country, and as the beauties of nature have hitherto been veiled from us by a succession of tunnels and cuttings, we welcome the landscapes which are presented to our view, as we begin to experience the exciting effect of railway travelling.

Passing through an open country, by an express or fast train, where the eye can embrace an uninterrupted view – the steady, but swift motion of the train imparts a peculiarly pleasing sensation, which may be compared to the sense of enjoying the changing scenes of a constantly varying panorama, without being required to perform the least effort or labour to obtain it.

The scenery now rapidly improves; passing Wormwood Scrubs on the left, we may notice the junction line of the North and South-Western Companies, curving towards the south. To the right appears some of the prettiest scenery in Middlesex; on the left is the rich foliage of Twyford Abbey – and before us expands the valley of the Brent.

WILLESDEN

Distance from station, 1 mile. Telegraph station at Kilburn, 3 miles. Money Order Office, 116, Edgeware Road.

The grave of the celebrated Jack Sheppard and his mother will be found in the churchyard, at this place.

The line now proceeds through fertile meads, the river Brent winding gracefully through the vale, and crossing this by a viaduct, we pass Apperton and Sudbury, to the south or left, and reach the station at

SUDBURY

Telegraph station at Harrow, 3 1/4 miles. Hotel – Swan. Money Order Office at Harrow.

Soon after leaving Sudbury we obtain a view of Harrow-on-the-Hill on the left, which, with its conspicuous church, becomes an interesting object in the landscape. The Harrow station is rather more than a mile from Harrow, lying in the vale below.

HARROW

Distance from station, 1 mile. A telegraph station.

Hotel – King's Head. Omnibuses to and from the station.

Post Horses, Flys, etc., at the station and hotels. Tariff – 1s. 6d. per mile.

Coaches to and from London, daily.

On account of the delightful prospect which the churchyard and summit of Harrow Hill affords, and the associations connected with Harrow, it is a place of frequent resort.

Crossing the meadow from the station we reach the foot of the hill, and if we ascend the summit, the view will be found to deserve all the encomiums bestowed upon it.

Harrow on the Hill

Above: A contemporary illustration of the long gradient with Harrow on the Hill to the right. The arrival of the railway was not without its perils and in the graveyard of St Mary's church there is a tombstone recording the death of Thomas Port, from a railway accident on 7 August 1838, barely a year since Euston had opened and a month before the through route to Birmingham was operational. The unfortunate Port was a guard on the L&BR and and slipped when attempting to climb down from his seat to the step boards on the outside of the carriages. He was dragged under the carriage and had both legs partially amputated. Harrow is better known for its school, now one of only four all-boys, full-boarding schools in Britain. Its alumni include eight former Prime Ministers, among them Baldwin, Palmerston, Peel, Baldwin and Churchill. *(LoC)*

The hill, rising almost isolated from an extensive plain, with the church and school on one side, and the old churchyard sloping on the other, forms in itself a combination of objects inexpressibly attractive and picturesque; but when the eye ranges over the vast expanse, and the landscape is lit up with the gorgeous and glowing sunset of a summer's eve, the prospect becomes extremely fascinating. It commands a delightful view of the wide, rich valley through which the Thames stretches its sinuous course; on the west it embraces a view of the fertile portions of Buckinghamshire and Berkshire; on the east London, with the dome of St Paul's; and to the south the towers of Windsor castle and the sweeping undulations of the Surrey hills. Harrow school was founded by John Lyon in the reign of Queen Elizabeth, and is still considered one of the first in the kingdom. The church contains a monument to Dr Drury, by Westmacott, on the north side of the nave, representing the schoolmaster seated, with two of his pupils studying beside him – the likenesses identifying them with the late Sir Robert Peel and Lord Byron, whose names have contributed to the interest attached to the locality. The poet in one of his letters describes the regard he had for a particular spot in the churchyard, where he used to sit for hours looking towards Windsor.

> As reclining at eve on yon tombstone he lay
> To catch the last gleam of the sun's setting ray.

Upon leaving Harrow station, we proceed over a slight ascent, passing Little Stanmore on the right – a small village, possessing an elegant little church, erected by the Chandos family.

Great Stanmore is two miles distant, and is situated on an eminence, adorned with handsome seats and villas.

After passing through a short cutting, the little village of Hatchend, which closely adjoins the railway on the right, appears pleasantly situated on the gentle slope of a hill. The bridge beneath, which we are now carried over, connects Hatchend with the village of Pinner, which, with the trees scattered around it, and the rich foliage of Pinner Park, forms a landscape of very considerable beauty.

PINNER

Distance from station, 1 mile. Telegraph station at Harrow, 2 miles.

Money Order Office at Harrow.

At this point we pass from Middlesex into

HERTFORDSHIRE

We cross the Oxley ridge, which forms a part of a chain of hills, and constitutes the boundary of the two counties. From this elevated position we have an opportunity of admiring the appearance of Hertfordshire.

There is no county of its size so rich in associations, and in stately seats of noblemen and gentlemen as the small inland county of Hertfordshire.

Picking up water

The LNWR's water trough at Bushey was the first one out of London and the most southern on the West Coast Main Line. Such troughs were a useful way of taking water without stopping the train. The Bushey trough, before the climb into the Chilterns, enabled the company to establish fast express services.

Top left: No. 46220, *Coronation* of the eponymous Coronation class, hauling the Royal Scot out of Euston. It began life with a streamlined exterior and in that form established a speed record of 114 mph, on the Euston to Glasgow run, in June 1937. Shown post-war in BR colours.

Middle left: LNWR Flying Scotsman taking water at Bushey troughs. *(CMcC)*

Below: No. 6201, *Princess Elizabeth* with Royal Scot. *(CMcC)*

York, Kent, and Surrey are only richer from their greater size. It is true that Herts has no cathedral; but she has St Alban's Abbey, one of the oldest and most instructive of all our mediaeval buildings; then she has Verulam, with its rich store of Roman remains; Gorhambury, sacred to the shade of the great Lord Bacon; Hatfield, rich in the wisdom of the Cecils; Panshanger, with its noble old oaks and picture gallery, second to none in Italian art in England; Cassiobury, with the pictures by Vandyke, Wilkie, Landseer, and Lely, and its woods and waters; the Grove, with that noble gallery of portraits formed by the great Lord Chancellor Clarendon; Moor Park, with its trees, not to be surpassed in England; Knebworth, with the Lytton associations and its Bulwer interest, etc.; and in conclusion Herts, with its sweet sylvan scenes, and trout streams – the Colne and the Chess.

To see the west side of Hertfordshire easily, an excursion tourist should get out at the Watford station.

Proceeding onward we enter the valley of the Colne, which forms a pretty landscape, and shortly after reach the station at

BUSHEY

Distance from station, ¾ mile. Telegraph station at , 1½ mile.

Money Order Office at Watford.

Just beyond Bushey, a handsome viaduct conducts us over the river Colne, and shortly after, we arrive at the Watford station, which is about a mile from the town.

WATFORD

Population, 4,385. A telegraph station. Hotel – Essex Arms.

Market Day – Tuesday. Fairs – March 31st, Aug. 29th and 30th, Sept. 9th.

Watford is a busy, thriving, and populous town, situated on the banks of the river Colne, and consists of only one street, with minor ones diverging from it. It is deficient in points of picturesque or antiquarian interest, but here are several places of attraction in the neighbourhood, viz – *Cassiobury Park*, the seat of the Earl of Essex, at whose instigation the tunnel at this place, 1,725 yards long, was suggested to the Railway Company; and *Grove Park*, the residence of the Earl of Clarendon.

A short branch turns off to the left. A little distance from the junction the line passes through the town of Watford, continuing its course to the town of

Rickmansworth, situated in the South Western extremity of the County of Herts, on the Grand Junction Canal. A good deal of straw-plait is manufactured here.

ST ALBANS BRANCH

Watford to St Albans

A run of seven miles from Watford, passing Bricket Wood, and leaving the little village of Park Street a little to the right, brings us to the town of

Top left: When the railways were new, the cuttings were laid bare as sculptural marks carved into the landscape without the cover of vegetation that has accumulated ever since. This is the approach to Watford Tunnel. Judging by the smoke the train appears to be travelling backwards.

Left: Watford North station in 2013. *(Cnbrb)*

Below: Siemens Class 350/1 Desiro, outer-suburban 4-car EMU No. 350 101 in the London Midland livery. On a Euston–Northampton service in July 2008. *(Hugh Llewelyn)*

ST ALBANS

Population, 7,675. A telegraph station. Hotels – Peahen, George.

Market Day – Saturday. Fairs – March 25th, 26th, October 10th and 11th.

Mails – Two arrivals and departures, daily, between London and St Albans.

Bankers – Branch of London and County Bank.

This ancient town of Herts, should be visited for its venerable abbey church, and that of St Michael's, which contains an excellent full-length statue of Lord Bacon, as he used to sit, thinking, in court. Bacon had a country house at Gorhambury, close by, and this figure of the 'greatest, wisest, mealiest of mankind', whose career is sketched with so much truth and reverence by Macaulay, in one of his best essays, was erected in the church, by Sir T. Meantys, or Mewtis, his admirer, as he calls himself; The *Abbey Church*, lately restored, is a cross-shaped pile, 539 feet long, exceeding most cathedrals, and interesting for the variety of styles it exhibits, its beautiful screen, tracery, painted ceiling, old brasses, &c., and the pillar of St Amphibalus, who converted St Alban, to whom King Offa, in 793, dedicated the priory. He is reckoned one of the earliest English martyrs, having suffered in 293, on Holmhurst Hill, close to the church. St Albans was the scene of two battles in the Wars of the Roses; the first in 1455, when Warwick, the king-maker, defeated Henry VI, and the other in 1461, when Margaret of Anjou routed Warwick. Many of those who fell were buried in the old church. It contains, also, the tombs of Good Duke Humphrey, and Matthew Paris, the historian. The body of Duke Humphrey (the same from whom dinner-hunters sometimes got an invitation), was found embalmed in pickle in 1703. Many Roman bricks or tiles, were used to rebuild this church, all collected from the spoils of *Verulamium*, one of the chief Roman cities In England; the sites of its walls, etc., are still traced, and relics frequently discovered. It was one of the places taken by Boadicea, in the time of Claudius, most of the inhabitants being put to the sword.

The gaol was the abbey gate-house. Much straw-plait is made here for the London market. Dame Juliana Berners, who wrote the *Book of St Albans*, the oldest work on hawking (1481), was abbess here; and there is a brass to her memory, the likeness on which, curiously enough, bears a great resemblance to a descendant of her family, in the present day, Lord Berners, of Didlington. At *Gorhambury*, now the seat of Earl Verulam, rebuilt in the last century, there are a few fragments of the old house which Lord Bacon's father erected.

L&NWR Main Line continued

Upon leaving the station at Watford, the train passes beneath a bridge, and a short distance beyond we enter the Watford Tunnel, and, on emerging therefrom, we continue for some time through an excavation, and, on the prospect opening on the left, we see the village of Langley Bury, a short distance from which is *Grove Park*, the seat of the Earl of Clarendon; and beautifully situated on the distant rising ground is the ancient village of King's Langley, so much frequented by King John. The Grand Junction Canal here runs close to the line, on the south of the embankment; and while the traveller looks with a smile of compassion upon the rival route we arrive at the station of

Above: A Southern class 377 EMU approaches Hemel Hempstead in August 2010, with a Milton Keynes to East Croydon service. *(Tom Walker)*

Left: J. C. Bourne's romanticised depiction of Stephenson's iron bridge over the Grand Junction Canal at Nash Mills, near King's Langley. 'From which the prospect is extensive and beautiful' Bradshaw tells us. When the lower photograph was taken in the 1930s the railway bridge had little changed.

KING'S LANGLEY

Population, 1,509. Telegraph station at Watford, 8 miles.

Mails – Two arrivals and departures, daily, between London and King's Langley.

Hotel – Rose and Crown.

The village of King's Langley on the right, Is remarkable for the square tower and short spire of its ancient church: there are several paper mills in the neighbourhood, that of the Messrs. Dickinson and Longman, at Two Waters, deserves a visit; good Ashing abounds. Several iron coffins were found here in 1840.

Proceeding onwards, the line crosses the King's Langley Viaduct, and thence by a bridge over the Grand Junction Canal, from which the prospect is extensive and beautiful. On the left is Moor Park, in the distance, and Primrose Green and King's Langley in the foreground. On the right, and near the line are Nash Mills, and a little further on a picturesque dingle, beyond which is *Gorhambury Park*, the seat of the Earl of Verulam. We thence pass through a short cutting, upon emerging from which, the village of Two Waters, and Corner Hall, surrounded with rich foliage, form a pleasing landscape. The line then enters a cutting nearly two miles long, on leaving which the train immediately arrives at the station at

BOXMOOR (Hemel Hempstead)

Telegraph station at Watford, 7 miles. Hotel – King's Arms.

Omnibuses to and from Hemel Hempstead.

Market Day – Thursday, at Hemel Hempstead. Fairs – Holy Thursday, Thursday after Trinity Sunday, and 3rd   Monday in September.

Money Order Office at Hemel Hempstead.

Bankers – Bucks & Oxon Union, and London & County.

Travellers would infer that this station derives its name from a moor in the vicinity; but the moor is at some distance, and the scenery in the neighbourhood of the station is exceedingly pretty and fertile. On leaving the station the line passes over an embankment, and the country becomes very interesting. To the left is Rowdown Common, with the richly wooded hills behind it, and on the right the village of Two Waters. The country is also interspersed with pretty cottages, with the church of Hemel Hempstead among the distant hills. *Westbrook Park*, the Hon. Dudley Ryder's seat, is in the vicinity.

Crossing the Box Lane Viaduct, the line runs parallel for some distance by the side of the Grand Junction Canal, which forms another agreeable feature in the picturesque scenery of this beautiful valley. Upon crossing the canal it proceeds along an embankment, which affords a fine prospect. We pass various hamlets on each side, and then reach the village of Bourne End on the left, where the embankment terminates; thence we pass through a cutting, on emerging from which we pass under Haxter's End Bridge, where the right-hand bank of the cutting terminates. On reaching Bank Mill Bridge a landscape of very great beauty bursts upon our view, including a view of the tower of Berkhampstead Church, the town itself, and the ruins of its ancient castle.

Above:
Berkhampstead
Castle represented
on the Town Hall
banner.

Left: The
newly opened
Berhampstead
station, and
the same scene
photographed in
the 1930s. The
canal is to the
right, although
largely hidden in
the later view.

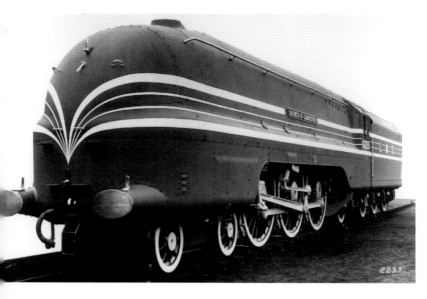

Bottom left:
The locomotive
shown in the
top picture is
one of the LMS
Coronation class.
These could
match the LNER's
A4 streamliners,
although some
critics suggest that
the streamlining
was largely done
for publicity
purposes. This
is the *Duchess of
Gloucester.*

Thence the line proceeds through a cutting, along an embankment, and arrives at the station of

BERKHAMPSTEAD

Population, 3,631. Telegraph station at Tring, 3¾ miles.

Hotel – King's Arms. Market Day – Saturday.

Fairs –Shrove Tuesday, Whit Monday, Michaelmas Tuesday and Wednesday.

Mails – Two arrivals and departures, daily, between London and Berhampstead.

Bankers – London and County Bank.

The elevated position of this station commands a delightful view of the valley on the left, in the bosom of which lies the town of Great Berkhampstead, where the author of the 'Task', the poet Cowper, was born, in 1731, and whose father was rector of this town. The church is cruciform, and as old as the cross. The beauties of the vale excite general admiration, and one cannot avoid remarking how singularly happy 'Nature' or the 'Muses' are in selecting the birthplaces of her favourite minstrels. What lovelier spot could be chosen to prompt the first accents of poetry than the groves and meads of this lovely valley. What could be more inspiring to the great bard than the scenery around Stratford-on-Avon; or where could a spot be found more adapted to inspire the muse of the Scottish minstrel, Burns, than the banks of the Doon?

Berkhampstead Castle, in ruins, was built soon after the Conquest, by Robert Montaigne.

After leaving this station we observe the houses of the town extend by the side of the line for some distance; whilst White Hill appears in the contrary direction. The line proceeds along the embankment, thence through a cutting into Northchurch Tunnel; on emerging from which we find ourselves again on an embankment, with a charming prospect on each side. *Ashbridge Park*, the seat of the Lady Alford, lies on the right. Passing alternately by embankment and cutting, we reach Wigginton Bridge, and obtain a view of the Chlltern Hills, the name of which is so familiar to us in connection with retiring members of parliament.

Tring Park is then seen to the left of the line, beautifully situated among hills, studded with trees, and containing a splendid mansion, built by Charles II, for the unfortunate Nell or Eleanor Gwynn, who caused that monarch to found Chelsea, and rebuild Greenwich Hospitals.

TRING

Population, 3,130. Distance from station, 1¾ mile.

A telegraph station. Hotels – King's Arms, Rose and Crown. Market Day – Friday.

Fairs – Easter Monday and Old Michaelmas Day Bankers – Butcher & Co.

At this station the railway reaches its greatest elevation, being 420 feet above the level of the sea, and 300 above that of Camden Town depot. This elevation is attained by a series of gradients never exceeding 1 in 300. The town of Tring has a handsome church containing some good monuments, and a curious enriched font.

CROSSING THE CHILTERN HILLS.
Tring Summit, on the Grand Junction Canal, the highest
water level in England, and
Tring Cutting, on the L.N.W. Railway, which is level with
the Dome of St. Paul's. *Photo,* NEWMAN, BERKHAMPSTED.

The cutting at Tring
One and a half million cubic yards of earth were
excavated from the Tring Cutting, where the
line crosses the Chilterns at 400 feet above sea
level. Taking over three years to make, when new
the exposed chalk of the cutting cut a gleaming
swathe of white through the green of the hills.
(CMcC)

Left: The line approaches Leighton Buzzard some
8 miles further on from Tring Cutting.

On leaving Tring station the line enters a deep cutting through the Chiltern Hills. This range of hills, once covered with woods, is part of a chain of hills extending from Norfolk (south-eastward) into Dorsetshire. They form at this point the northern basin of the Colne, and separate it from that part of Buckingham which is designated the vale.

Upon issuing from this cutting a great extent of country becomes visible on both sides of the line, which now passes from the county of Hertford into

BUCKINGHAMSHIRE

The face of this county is much varied; the fertile vale of Aylesbury spreads through the middle of the county, and furnishes a rich pasture to vast numbers of cattle. The natural fertility of this vale has been highly extolled, and is almost unrivalled. It lies between the Chiltern Hills and a parallel range of hills, running at a distance of only a few miles along the western side of Buckinghamshire.

Proceeding along the side of the canal, we have on our left Cheddington Hill, which conceals the village of Cheddington from our view.

CHEDDINGTON (Junction)

Population, 628. Distance from station, ½ mile.

Telegraph station at Tring, 4¼ miles. Money Order Office at Tring, 4¼ miles.

From this station a branch rail, seven miles long, turns off on the left to Aylesbury, which we will describe, and then continue our progress with the main line.

AYLESBURY BRANCH

Mansion Gate station.

AYLESBURY

Population, 27,090. Telegraph station at Tring, 11¼ miles. Hotels – George, White Hart. Omnibuses to and from Prince's Risboro' daily. Coaches to Thame, daily.

Market Day – Saturday. Fairs – Jan. 18th, May 8th, June 14th, Oct. 11th, on which occasion the farmers hire all their servants from year to year, Sept. 25th, and Saturday before Palm Sunday.

The town of Aylesbury, for the accommodation of which this line was formed, is nine miles west of the main line, delightfully situated in a fertile vale, which affords pasturage to an extraordinary number of sheep. It derives its importance chiefly from its being the mart for the produce of the rich vale in which it is situate.

It is an agricultural town and borough (returning two members), in Bucks. It stands on a low hill in the rich vale of Aylesbury, a loose tract of luxuriant grass land, in the centre of the county, worth £25 an acre. Chalk Hills bound it to the north and south. Drayton describes it as 'Dusty, firm, and fat'.

Aylesbury was a Saxon manor, which William the Conqueror granted to one of his followers, on the tenure of finding straw for his bed, three eels, and three green geese.

Left: Brilliantly labelled by the locals as the 'Blue Leanie', this modern office building for HBOS is in Aylesbury. *(Michael Jamieson)*

Lower left: Wonderfully free of traffic, a postcard view of Temple Square and Church Street in Aylesbury, *c.* 1905. *(CMcC)*

Below: An 1873 illustration of the famous Aylesbury Ducks. These were bred and force-fed for the Christmas table.

Below: The wide Vale of Aylesbury as photographed from Whipsnade Zoo. Bradshaw tells us that it is, 'a fertile vale, which affords pasturage to an extraordinary number of sheep'. *(Martin Pettitt)*

For many generations it belonged to the Packingtons, who had such hold on the town, that Dame Packington, in Elizabeth's time, by letter appointed 'my trusty and well-beloved so-and-so to be my burgessors from said time' promising to ratify and approve what they did at Westminster, as fully as if she were present there herself. In 1804 it was so notorious for bribery that the voting was extended to the whole hundred. Before this (in 1702) one Ashby brought an action against White, the returning officer, for refusing his vote. He obtained a verdict, which the Court of Queon's Bench reversed; but, upon appeal, the House of Lords finally decided in his favour. The Commons, in consequence of that, claimed the sole right of judging how members were to be elected, and declared Ashby guilty of a breach of privilege in appealing to any tribunal but theirs, and sent its attorney to Newgate. The case being taken up by the House of Lords, led to some violent proceedings on the part of the Commons, which were terminated only by a prorogation. A similar attempt was made by the Commons, in the case of Stockdale the printer, in 1832. At present the supremacy of the regular courts of law is established, and no assertion of privilege would be allowed to contravene public right.

Like most old country towns, it is irregularly built. A small branch of the Thames runs through it to that river, which is 2 miles off. Here are the brick county hall, where the county members are nominated; lodgings for the judges in their circuit, lately built by E. Lamb; a town hall and market house, rebuilt on the site of an ancient pile, in the Grecian style, copied from the Temple of the Winds at Athens, which was of eight sides, facing the principal points of the compass; and a well-endowed grammar school.

The church (in a large churchyard) is a decorated English cross, with a low tower, overlooking the vale, and seen from most parts of it. There is a carved pulpit, and tombs of the Lees of Quorendon, an ancient seat, 2 miles north. The vicarage is on the site of a monastery to St Osyth, who was born here. She was martyred, and gives name to Size Lane, London.

Lace and straw-plait are made here; but another manufacture peculiar to the town is ducklings, which are forced for the Christmas market. The ducks are kept from laying till about October or November, when they are fed with abundance of stimulating food, and hens employed to sit on the eggs. The young brood being hatched are nursed with great care, opposite a fire, and fetch 15s. or 20s. a couple at Christmas. As many as three quarters of a million ducks are sent to London from this part.

Within a few miles are several seats. *Hartwell*, that of Dr Lee, was, in the late war, the residence of Louis XVIII and his family. *Wooton*, belonging to the Duke of Buckingham, has been in that family (the Grenville) since the Conquest. *Weedon* is the Duke of Marlborough's. *Lillies* was the seat of the late Lord Nugent (a Grenville). Further off, on the Banbury Road, is *Wootton Underwood*, consecrated to the memory of Cowper, who lived here with his cousin, Lady Hesketh, near the Throckmorton's old seat. The poet's house is standing. It was while living here, at the close of his life, that he produced his Homer (1791).

L&NWR Main Line continued

LNWR's high-speed train

Built in 1873, *Hardwicke* is a 2-4-0 of the Improved Precedent class designed by F. W. Webb for main line passenger services from Euston to the north-west. In 1895 it set a new speed record during a period of intense rivalry between the LNWR and the GNR – known as the 'Race to the North' – when it covered the 141 miles between Crewe and Carlisle in 2 hours 6 minutes. Withdrawn in 1932, it is now at the National Railway Museum in York.

Cheddington to Leighton Junction

The line crosses Aylesbury Vale by an embankment, which is 25 feet in height, and affords an extensive view in every direction. Several pretty villages are scattered over the valley and slopes; and after crossing the Horton Viaduct, we catch a glimpse of the spire of Leighton Buzzard Church, and the country beyond, and shortly after of that town itself. We proceed by alternate embankment and cutting past several beautiful views, and then reach

LEIGHTON JUNCTION (Leighton Buzzard)

> A telegraph station. Hotels – Swan, Unicorn. Market Day – Tuesday. Fairs – Feb. 5th, Whit Tuesday, July 26th, Oct. 24th, and second Tuesday in December.

This small market town, of 4,930 inhabitants, who make lace, and straw-plait, is situated in Bedfordshire. The branch to Dunstable turns off here; and the Ouzel, a branch of the Ouse, divides the town from Bucks and the chalk hills on the west. These hills are part of the range which, in south Bucks, run through the Chiltern Hundred, giving name to a nominal office, by which an MP is enabled to vacate his seat. Leighton *Church* is a good Gothic cross, with stalls (for the priests of one or two priory-cells, that were here), and a tall spire, 193 feet high, before about 25 feet was struck down by lightning, 10th July, 1852. Its ancient Cross near the market house, also deserves notice, as a genuine relic of early English work, built about 1300, and stands 34 feet high on 5 steps, and set off with pinnacles and niches.

In the neighbourhood are the following places. Stewkley, and its excellent *Norman Church*, on the Chiltern hills, *Liscombe House*, Lady Lovett, the old Elizabethan seat of an ancient family. *Aston Abbot's House*, seat of Sir James Ross, the Polar navigator, *Wing Park*, Lord Overstone the banker. Whaddon, on the hills, once the centre of a large chase or forest. *Great Brickhill*, Hon. P. Buncombe.

DUNSTABLE BRANCH

Leighton to Dunstable

A branch rail, seven miles long, turns off on the right from Leighton Buzzard to Dunstable, in Bedfordshire.

DUNSTABLE

> Population, 4,470. Telegraph station at Leighton, miles.
> Hotels – White Hart, King's Head, Railway. Market Day – Wednesday.
> Fairs – Ash Wednesday, 22nd May, August 12th, and November 12th.

Dunstable is situated at the foot of the Chiltern hills. The principal attraction of this town was its ancient priory church, and the celebrity of its inns. It is noted for straw-plait manufacture. Many of the houses have an antiquated appearance, and the streets,

Code breakers at Bletchley

During the Second World War, Allied signals intelligence – designated Ultra – played a crucial role in decyphering Nazi Germany's Enigma and Lorenz codes. A secret team of MI6 cryptanalysts was assembled well away from London at a mansion in Buckinghamshire. This was Bletchley Park, the Government Code and Cypher School.

Top left and above: The Enigma machine used alphabet rotors to create almost unbreakable codes. *(Ted Coles/CIA)*

Left: Bletchley is now a museum and visitors can see the reconstructed Colussus computer as well as the codebreakers' huts and Engima machines. *(Jay Christopher)*

which are four in number, take the direction of the four cardinal points, Intersecting each other at right angles.

The town lies among chalk hills, on the site of a Roman station on Watling Street. It has a large priory church, partly Norman.

London and North Western Main Line continued

Leighton to Bletchley Junction

Upon leaving Leighton, the line passes over a level country for nearly fifteen miles, but has occasionally to go through a tunnel or cutting in its course. At this distance it makes a curve, and on reaching the open country Linslade Wood is soon on both sides, and Linslade Hall and Church to the right. A short distance beyond is the town of Great Brickhill, standing on one of the hills which lie to the right. In the same direction is Stoke Hammond; and on the left are Stewkley, Soulbury, and Liscombe Park. The church of Stewkley is one of the most enriched and perfect specimens of Norman architecture now existing. From this point the scenery improves, the hills are studded with trees, and the landscape is of a very pleasing character. The train next reaches

BLETCHLEY

Population, 426. Distance from station, ¼ mile. A telegraph station.

From the peculiar position of this station it affords a most extensive prospect of the line of railway, and of the surrounding country, embracing the town of Bletchley, Drayton Parslow on the left, and in the distance may be seen Whaddon Chace and Hall, in which Queen Elizabeth was entertained by Arthur Lord Grey.

To the right of the station, and standing on a hill, is the small town of Fenny Stratford. The village of Water Eaton is seen in the foreground in the same direction, and on the wooded hills which rise beyond, the three Brickhills are still discernible. From the Bletchley station branch rails turn off on the left to Winslow, Oxford, and Banbury, and on the right to Bedford, both of which lines we will here describe.

BEDFORD BRANCH

Bletchley to Bedford and Cambridge

The first station on this Branch being partly in the parish of Bletchley is quickly announced.

FENNY STRATFORD

Population, 1,109. Distance from the station, ¼ mile. Telegraph station at Bletchley, 1¼ mile. Market Day – Monday. Fairs – April 19th, July 18th, October 10th November 28th. Mails – Two arrivals and departures, daily between London and Fenny Stratford.

Bradshaw can be excused for not knowing that Newport Pagnell would become the spiritual home of Britain's greatest automotive marque, Aston Martin. *(JC)*

Woburn Abbey, Bedfordshire, as it was, left, and the rebuilt version dating from 1744, below. It is the main family home of the Duke of Bedford, and along with the safari park it is open to the public. *(Viki Male)*

Fenny Stratford is in a once fenny part of the Ouzel, on the Watling Street, or Roman way, which crosses the Ouse, further on, at Stony Stratford, where Richard III seized his poor little nephew, Edward V. Lace and plait are made at both places. The Ouse, as it sluggishly winds down to Newport Pagnell,

> Now glitters in the sun, and now retires.
> As bashful yet impatient to be seen. – *Cowper*

Much lace and some paper are made at Newport Pagnell; in the church is an epitaph by Cowper. *Gayhurst*, the seat of Lord Carrington, 2 miles to the north-west, is an antique Elizabethan house, and has a portrait of Sir Kenelm Digby, who was born here, 'a prodigy of learning, credulity, valour, and romance.' *Hanslope*, on a hill, lies an old Gothic church, with, a spire 190 feet high. Olney, another town of lace-makers, with the house in which *Cowper* lived till 1786.

> Yon Cottager that weaves at her own door,
> Pillow and bobbins all her little store;
> Content though mean, etc. – Cowper's *Truth*.

Scott the commentator, and John Newton, were curates of Olney, and the latter, in conjunction with Cowper, here wrote his well known Olney hymns.

WOBURN SANDS

Population, 1,349. Distance from the station, 2 miles.
Telegraph station at Bletchley, 4¼ miles. Hotel – Bedford Arms.
Market Day – Friday. Fairs – January 1st, March 23rd, July 13th, September 25th.

Woburn – situated on a gentle eminence – is surrounded with plantations and evergreens, and consists of four broad streets, which intersect each other at right angles. In the centre of the town is a noble market house, erected by the Duke of Bedford, in the Tudor style of architecture. The church is covered with ivy, and has a remarkably beautiful appearance.

In the immediate vicinity of the town is *Woburn Abbey*, the seat of the Duke of Bedford. It is a modern quadrangular building, handsome, but heavy. The west front has four Ionic columns, and the east four fluted Doric ones. The interior contains a large gallery of portraits, and a collection of Italian and Dutch paintings; and in the pleasure ground is a sculpture gallery formed by the present Duke which contains a group of the Graces, by Canova, which cost £3,000. The park is twelve miles in circuit, and contains a large herd of deer.

Immediately after leaving this station we take our leave of the county of Bucks, and enter that of

BEDFORD

Victorian Bedford
Two photochrom views of the county town from around 1895.

Above: The bridge and promenade with pleasure boats on the River Ouse. *(LoC)*

Left: The bronze statue of the philanthropist John Howard, who is credited as being the first prison reformer, in St Paul's Square in Bedford. It was deigned by Sir Alfred Gilbert – creator of the Eros statue in Piccadilly Circus – and erected in 1894. As a sickly child Howard had lived in Cardington for a time, and in later life he settled there. In 1773 he was appointed High Sheriff of Bedfordshire. *(LoC)*

The surface, on the north and east, and in the fruitful vale of Bedford, is generally flat; but on the south-west, the chalk hills run to a considerable height, affording many fine prospect – as at Ampthill, Woburn, and Millbrook, which command an extent of 50 miles. The greatest part is enclosed, and an improved system of agriculture has been adopted. The farms average 200 acres, and let yearly. The stock of cattle is reckoned at 200,000, and the supply of wool, 4,250 packs. The only manufactures peculiar to the county are the pillow lace and straw plait.

Ridgemont and Lidlington stations.

AMPTHILL

Population, 2,011. Telegraph station at Bedford, 5¾ miles.

Ampthill Park, Lord Holland's seat, 1½ mile from the station, was the residence of Queen Catherine after her divorce from Henry VIII. The sentence was pronounced by Cranmer in Dunstable Church. There is an inscription to her memory by Horace Walpole, the point of which is:

> From Catherine's wrongs a nation's bliss was spread,
> And Luther's light from Henry's lawless bed.

BEDFORD

A telegraph station. Hotels – Swan; George. Omnibuses to and from the station; also to Kimbolton, on Tuesdays, Fridays, and Saturdays. Market Days – Tuesday and Saturday. Fairs – April 21st, July 5th. August 21st. Oct 11th, Dec. 19th, first Tuesday in Lent. Bankers – Branch of London and County Bank; T. Barnard and Son.

The agricultural capital of *Bedfordshire*, 16 miles from Bletchley, at the terminus of a branch from the North Western line. The sedgy Ouse runs through the town, which takes its name from a *ford*, guarded by a castle of the Beauchamps, when William the Conqueror gained military possession of the country. A good stone bridge now crosses it. Population, 13,413. Two members returned to parliament. Pillow lace, shoes, and straw plait are made. St Paul's is the most remarkable of its six Gothic churches, and contains the effigy of a Beauchamp, and a monument to Lord Mayor Harpur, who was born here, and the founder of an extensive charity, to which is attached the celebrated Bedford Schools, open to all inhabitants of the town, well conducted, and amply endowed for boys and girls, and 70 or 80 alms-houses, besides distributing apprentice fees, and marriage portions, and now possessing a revenue of £2,000 per annum from land in Holborn and his native town. Being open to all, it has the effect of drawing many families to the town.

At Mill Lane Chapel *John Bunyan* preached, for which he was cast into gaol (on the site of the county prison), where he wrote his *Pilgrim's Progress*. The immortal tinker was born in 1628, at Elstow, 1½ mile south, past the asylum. His cottage and forge are there, while his chair is preserved in the chapel.

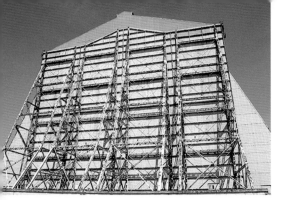

Two huge airship sheds dominate the higher ground at Cardington, relics of the former Shorts Bros. works that became the focal point for Britain's Imperial Airship Scheme in the 1920s. Several airships were built here, including *R101*. Its sister ship, *R100*, was designed by Barnes Wallis and built at Howden, Yorkshire, before coming to Cardington. The main picture shows the *R101* chopped in half to increase its volume. *Left:* Members of the crew at the base of the mooring mast with the *R101* behind. *(JC)*

One of the oldest houses in Bedford is the George Inn, a remnant of the 15th century.

Within a distance of 5 or 6 miles are – *Kempston House*, seat of R. Newland. Esq; *Bramham Hall*, seat of the Trevors; *Newnham Priory* ruins; and *Oakley House*, belonging to the Marquis of Tavistock, a building of Charles II's time; *Howbury*, the Polhills' seat.

Blunham Station.

SANDY

A telegraph station. Hotel – Greyhound. Money Order Office at Biggleswade, 3 miles.

Sandy, the ancient Salina, was formerly a military station, surrounded with ramparts, and to the north-east is an immense hill called Caesar's Camp, supposed to have been the spot where the Conqueror encamped, after sailing up the river Ivel, from Lyne. On the top of this hill is a beautiful walk. The gardeners in this neighbourhood send large supplies of vegetables, especially cucumbers, to the London market. The railway now runs in the direction of the river Ouse, leaving the town of Eaton Socon on the left. About three miles distant is the market town of Potton, at which fairs are held in January, 3rd Tuesday; April, last Tuesday; July, 1st Tuesday; October, Tuesday before the 29th. Also, near at hand are Sutton Park, the seat of Sir J. Burgoyne, Bart.; and Sandy Park, Hon. Mrs Ongley, where coins have been found of an ancient date.

Passing the stations of Gamlingay, Old North Road, and Lord's Bridge, we very soon cross the River Cam, when the arrival of the train is announced at Cambridge.

BLETCHLEY AND OXFORD BRANCH

Bletchley to Winslow and Oxford

SWANBOURNE.

Population, 603. Distance from station, 1 mile. Telegraph station at Winslow, .2 miles. Money Order Office at Winslow.

WINSLOW

Population, 1,890. Distance from station, ¼ mile. A telegraph station.
Hotel – The Bell Market Day – Thursday. Fairs – March 20, Holy Thursday, August 21st, September 22nd, Thursday before October 11th.

BANBURY BRANCH

Winslow to Buckingham and Banbury

A distance of seven miles beyond the junction at Winslow brings us to the town of

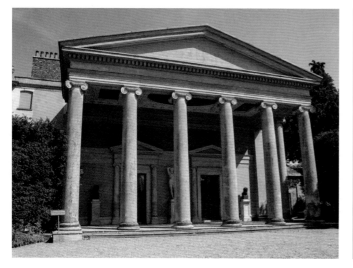

CAMEL CALF
Born at Uxbridge, on Wednesday, February 13th, 1907, during the visit of Messrs. Bostock & Wombwell's Menagerie.

Above: Typical scene of a man with camel calf – a postcard published by the *Middlesex & Buckinghshire Advertiser* in 1907. *(CMcC)*

Top left: West Wycombe Park, now a National Trust property. *(Simon)*

Left: Watling Street in Towcester, pronounced 'toaster', a small town just 8 miles to the south-west of Northampton. *(Cj1340)*

Bottom left: Silverstone racing circuit is only 5 miles from Towcester. It is the current home of the British Grand Prix, which it first hosted in 1948. This photograph shows the WEC (World Endurance Championship) Silverstone 6 Hours in 2013. *(David Merrett)*

BUCKINGHAM

Distance from station, ¼ mile. A telegraph station. Hotel – White Hart.

Market Day – Saturday.Fairs – Monday fortnight after the Epiphany, March 6th, May 6th, July 10th, Sept. 4th, Oct. 2nd, Nov. 8th, Saturday after Old Michaelmas, Whit-Thursday. Bankers – Bartlett, Parrott, and Co.; Branch of London & County Bank.

Buckingham has a population of 7,626: agriculture and lace making occupy their attention. The church, built in 1781, on the site of a castle, has rather a pretty appearance – the spire is 150 feet. A beautiful painting of Raphael's Transfiguration, the gift of the Duke of Buckingham, decorates the altar. At a distance of two miles from here is *Stowe*, the late magnificent residence of the Duke of Buckingham. It is a noble structure, in the Grecian style, designed by Lords Camelford and Cobham. Its internal decorations, consisting of works of art in plate, furniture, etc., were of the most costly description, and these, together with a library of 10,000 volumes, a large collection of MSS., portraits and engravings, with the principal family estates, were sold by auction in 1848, to pay off a mortgage debt of one and a half million.

We now pass through fine country for about seven miles, watered by the river Ouse, over which the rails frequently cross. We then enter the county of Northampton, upon which the arrival of the train is announced at

BRACKLEY

Distance from station, ¼ mile. A telegraph station. Hotel – Wheat Sheaf.

Market Day – Wednesday. Fairs – December 11th, Wednesday after Feb. 25th, Oct. 10th, and 2nd Wednesday in April.

This place has a population of 2,239: staple manufacture, lace and shoes. It is one of the oldest boroughs in the kingdom, and contains some relics of its former state. Brackley gives the title of viscount to the Earl of Ellesmere.

We are now traversing the south western section of the fox-hunting county of Northampton, and, at the distance of 4¾ miles, arrive at the station of Farthinghoe, in the vicinity of which the river Ouse takes its rise. Four miles further brings us to

Banbury, in the county of Oxford.

Winslow to Oxford

CLAYDON

Population, 385. Distance from station, ¼ mile. Telegraph station at Winslow, 4 miles. Money Order Office at Winslow, 4 miles.

Launton station.

Wolverton workshop
Bradshaw enthuses at some length on the LNWR works established in 1838 at the midpoint between London and Birmingham. *Left:* Seen from the opposite side of the Grand Junction Canal, plus Stephenson's iron girder bridge. *(Peter Lewis) Above:* Workshop in 2007. *(John Maynard Friedman) Below:* Planet class loco of 1830, formerly with Liverpool & Manchester Railway and later the LNWR. *(CMcC)*

BICESTER

Population, 2,798. Distance from station, ¼ mile. A telegraph station. Hotels – King's Anns; Crown. Market Day – Friday. Fairs – Friday in Easter week, Whit Monday, first Friday in June, August 5th October 10th, and December 11th.

Bankers – Henry Michael, and George Tubb.

ISLIP

Population, 688. Telegraph station at Oxford, 6 miles.

Money Order Offices at Oxford and Bicester, 6 miles.

L&NWR Main Line continued

Bletchley to Blisworth

Upon leaving Bletchley we pass through a cutting, and cross the London road by an iron bridge, and proceeding onwards we arrive in view of the churches of Loughton and Shewston, the latter of which is a fair specimen of the Norman style of architecture. Near the line on the right is the village of Bradwell, and thence after a short cutting we reach the station at

WOLVERTON

Distance from station, 5 mile. A telegraph station.

Hotels – Swan, Cock. Refreshment room at station.

Omnibuses to and from Newport Pagnell, and Stoney Stratford, twice daily.

Wolverton, near the river Ouse, has an increasing population of 2,370, chiefly dependent on the London and North Western Railway Company, who have a depot and extensive factories here. It is also a refreshment station. A new church and market house, and hundreds of model cottages, have been built by the Company, whose works cover 12 acres of ground. While Crewe is the nursery, Wolverton is the hospital for locomotives. There are the worn-out, the ricketty, the accidents, and sundry other wards, in all of which locomotives are to be seen undergoing cure. Red hot pieces of iron are being forcibly administered; holes probed and nuts screwed on them; steam lathes are facing down callosities; hundreds of locomotive surgeons – stalwart and iron-fisted – dress and bind up cases in their wards with a tremendous energy. Sickly-looking locomotives are fitted up with brand new outsides; several in the last stages of collapse have strong doses of copper rivets forced into their systems. Metal giants, shaky about the knees, are furnished with new sets of joints. In the most desperate cases a cure is effected. Ninety-nine out of every hundred of these battered patients come out perfectly restored to their bereaved stokers. By the help of a blast furnace and steam hammer, even the most incurable is beaten young again, and reproduced as a new locomotive, called perhaps the *Phoenix* – (*Household Words*, 1853). Nothing is wasted here, for the scraps are welded together in the furnace, for axles or cranks, or any other duty requiring temper and strength. The metal cutting and planing works deserve notice.

Left: Wolverton viaduct, spanning the River Ouse, is 660 feet long and cost the not inconsiderable sum of £28,000 to build. Bradshaw describes it as a 'remarkable and beautiful structure'.

Above and left: Prior to September 1838, the line from London terminated at a temporary station at Denbigh Hall Bridge while the Kilsby Tunnel was being completed. Passengers proceeded by coach to Rugby to rejoin the railway. The photograph of the bridge is from the 1930s.

Proceeding onwards from Wolverton the train conveys us through a beautifully diversified country. First the lofty spire of Hanslope church is seen, then Bradwell Wharf, Linford, and Mill Mead, appear on the right, and the village of Wolverton on the left, shortly after which we arrive at the far-famed viaduct over the Ouse valley. This remarkable and beautiful structure consists of six arches of sixty-feet span, In addition to six smaller ones placed in the abutments. The viaduct presents a noble and magnificent appearance to a person in the valley; and the view from the train in passing over it is exceedingly fine.

After the termination of the Wolverton embankment, we pass through a short cutting, and then proceed along another embankment, through some finely wooded country, interspersed with hill, vale, and picturesque villages. The scenery on the left retains the same characteristic for miles. The country surrounding Stoney Stratford forms a fine rear view; and Stoke Park adds to the beauties of the landscape.

Immediately after coming within sight of these parks we cross the boundary line between Buckinghamshire and

NORTHAMPTON

And enter the latter county, which has for centuries been proverbial for its beauty, and the number of its resident gentry. It is distinguished from the neighbouring counties by the extensive forests and private woodlands that are scattered over the face of the county, and add so much to the beauty and picturesque effect of its scenery. The ground on the whole rises towards the north and north west, and presents a sort of inclined plane towards the south eastern extremity of the county, where the river Nene traverses nearly through its whole length, which, generally speaking, rises in the high pounds, and descends in a variety of streams, diffusing their beneficial influence with singular effect over the whole county. Northamptonshire may justly boast, and we believe exclusively, that in the important article of water it is completely independent; for of the six rivers which flow through or intersect it, every one originates within its boundaries, and not a single brook, however insignificant, runs into it from any other district. The climate of Northamptonshire is mild, and the air exceedingly pure, healthy, and favourable to vegetation. The soil is various, but on the whole fertile and productive. The county is also intersected by several of the most important canals in the kingdom.

The entrance of the line into the county is known by some pretty thatched cottages, which stand on each side of the line, and constitute the village of Ashton. Here the embankment, which has extended nearly a mile, and afforded so many delightful views of the surrounding country comes to a termination. After passing through three moderate cuttings we reach the station at

ROADE

Formation, 644. Telegraph station at Wolverton, 7¾ miles.

Money Order Office at Northampton.

The village of Roade is situated on the right of the line, but presents no object requiring

Left: The bridge over the road at Blisworth. In Stephenson's times and more recently in 2007. It has little changed although the artist of the earlier image has deliberately exaggerated its height. *(Cj1340)*

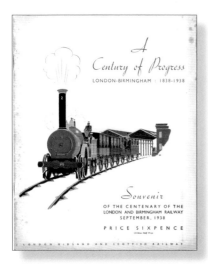

A Century of Progress

In September 1938 the LMS celebrated the centenary of the London & Birmingham Railway and several of the illustrations in this book are taken from the special Souvenir. 'In pursuing through the difficult years that followed its formation [in 1923] a progressive policy to improve its service to the public in all phases of its activity the LMS is perpetuating the forward spirit that emboldened its ancestor whose centenary we now celebrate.' But the celebrations were to be short-lived. The war was looming on the horizon, and when peace came the nation's worn and battered railways were nationalised.

notice. Shortly after leaving this station we enter an excavation made through the Blisworth ridge, when the open country is again visible. The most interesting scenery lies on the right. Hunsbury Hill, Bury Wood, and Harpole Hills, with Wooton, among the hills, and the prominent village of Milton, or Middleton, and its neat church, form a landscape of no ordinary beauty. Immediately preceding our arrival at Blisworth Junction we perceive the pretty village of Blisworth, situated on the gentle sloping ground on the right.

Blisworth Junction.

NORTHAMPTON AND PETERBOROUGH BRANCH

Blisworth to Northampton and Peterborough

The line turns off to the right; and commences in a curve over a bridge across the Grand Junction Canal, where a fine view of the surrounding country obtained.

NORTHAMPTON

Distance from station, ½ mile. A telegraph station. Hotels – Angel, George, Peacock, Market Days – Wednesday and Saturday. Fairs – The 2nd Tuesday in January, Feb. 20th, the 3rd Monday in March, April 5th, May 4th, June 19th, Aug. 5th, Aug. 26th, Sept. 19th, the first Thursday in November, Nov. 28th, and the Friday before Smithfield Great Market. Bankers – Northampton Union; Northamptonshire Banking Company. Races – Pytchley Hunt, in March. Cricket Club in June.

Northampton is a borough town, standing on the banks of the river Nene, on the left of the line. It is memorable in the annals of political and local history, for the number of synods and councils held within its walls, its formidable castle and provincial earls, its numerous monastic foundations, military events, and last, not least, for the many important Improvements which it has undergone within the last half century.

The capital of Northamptonshire, one of the chief towns in the Midland counties, and a parliamentary borough, returning two members, with an industrious population of 32,813, some thousands of whom are engaged in the boot and shoe manufacture, which has been noted here for centuries. The trade indeed is so flourishing, that there is a saying, 'You may know when you are within a mile of Northampton by the sound of the cobler's lapstone.' Formerly it was celebrated for its leather bottles, so that St Crispin has always been its patron saint. The George Inn was given by the Drydens towards the support of their blue-coat school. It was one of two important *hamptons* in Saxon times, which since the Doomsday survey, have been called Northampton and Southampton, and are still prosperous and increasing towns. It is on the river Nene, and the Northampton and Peterborough Railway, 67 miles from London, via Blisworth, on the North Western, From 1138, in Henry I's reign, to 1380, as many as 20 parliaments were held here, showing its pre-eminence at that period. One of the most important, as regards our constitutional progress, was that called by Henry II, in 1170, when the towns were ordered to send burgesses for the first time. One held five years before,

Northampton

Top left: The grand Guildhall. *(Tony Hisgett)* The town was renowned for its shoe and boot makers. The image on the left presents a somewhat romanticicsed view of a man and boy making shoes in a painting by Emilie Adan, *c.* 1914. The reality was more likely to be a 'manufactory', as shown at bottom left.

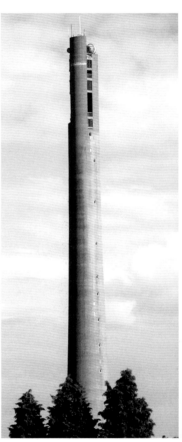

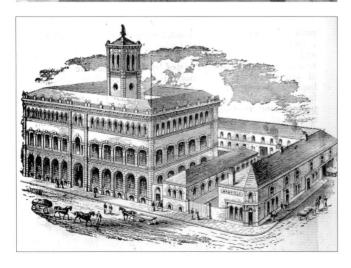

Above: The locals call it the Nottingham Lighthouse. Completed in 1982, this 418-foot edifice is the National Lift Tower, previously the Express Lift Tower, and was used to test the company's products. *(G-Man)*

confirmed the Constitution of Clarendon, which subjected clergy to the common laws, and led to à Becket's rebellion. On another occasion, when disputes occurred at Oxford, the University was moved hither, but only for a time. A great fire in 1675 destroyed 500 houses. It is a clean, neatly built town on a gentle slope, with houses of reddish stone. The most bustling quarters are the Drapery, and the large open Market Place near it, round which All Saints Church, the Corn Exchange, Town Hall, Bank, George and Peacock Hotels, etc., are grouped.

All Saints, close to George Row, is a modern building, except the tower, which was built in the 13th century. Above the Grecian portico is the statue of Charles II, in a Roman toga, and a French wig. It contains a painting by Thornhill, Chantrey's statue of Spencer Perceval, the premier who was assassinated by Bellingham in the House of Commons' lobby, in 1812, a well carved screen and pulpit, one of Hill's large organs (3,000 pipes), and part of the old crypt; an ancient conduit stood at one corner of the churchyard. In the north aisle is the figure of a charity girl, executed by S. Cox, to whom Cowper refers in his letters. When the parish clerk applied for verses to affix to the bills of mortality, the poet told him, 'there is a namesake of yours, Cox the statuary, who everybody knows is a first-rate maker of verses; he surely is the man for your purpose.' 'Ah, Sir,' says the clerk, 'I have heretofore borrowed his help, but he is a gentleman of so much reading that the people of our town cannot understand him.' It was from calculations founded on these annual bills that Dr Price derived his tables, which are in use at some of the Old Life Assurance Offices. They are, however, much less in favour of the assurers than subsequent tables. In St John's Lane, near Bridge, is the old Hospital of St John, first founded about 1170, by the St Liz family. The cotton mill near this, now occupied by a miller, was first designed for spinning cotton. Close to South Gate is another old hospital, founded in 1450, in honour of à Becket; it is now replaced by a new house in St Giles Street.

St Giles Street leads to St Giles Church, formerly a Norman cross, of which the door remains; there are signs of later styles, and of three roofs preceding the one in existence. The old east gate of the town stood near this; and beyond are the Union Workhouse, the new Cemetery (opened in 1846), and the Courtly Asylum, a plain but striking building of great size, on a site of 24 acres, built in 1836, of Bath stone. There is a good view from it of Delapre, Abbey, etc., to the South.

The Town Hall, at Wood Hill Corner, contains a portrait of Perceval (who once resided here), by Joseph. At the corner of Market Square, adjoining Newland, is an old house, with shields on the front, in which are the arms borne by the Meredyths and other Welsh families, the motto Heb dhuw (or dyw) heb dyw, Dhuw a digon, i.e., 'without God, without everything; God, and enough' – a truly noble sentiment, the essence of Christian philosophy. The County Gaol, built by Milne, on the model system, was opened in 1846, for 160 prisoners; it adjoins the Shire Hall (which contains portraits of sovereigns from William III), and the judges' lodgings, in the Grecian style. There is a good library at the Religious and Useful Knowledge Society's Rooms, in Gold Street, also at the Mechanics' Institute, at the new Corn Exchange.

In the new Corn Exchange, built in 1851, by Alexander, is a noble hall, 140 feet long; here the Athenaeum and Library are placed, In Sheep Street, opposite the Ram Inn, stood the famous nonconformist academy, carried on by Doddridge, which, upon his death at Lisbon, was moved to Daventry, in 1752. There is a monument of this excellent man at Castle Hill Chapel, where he was minister for the last 22 years of his life. The General Library, established in 1800, is close to the Mercury office, a paper started by the Dicey family, as far back as 1720.

Up Sheep Street, you come to the Royal Terrace, and the barracks, built in 1796. The large Race Ground (117 acres), is beyond. Here the Pytchley Hunt races are held in March, and the cricket club in summer. In this quarter also is the Roman Catholic chapel of St Felix, built in 1844, by Pugin, in the Gothic style, with a nunnery and bishop's house attached. But the most noticeable building is the ancient church of St Sepulchre, one of the four remaining churches in England, built by the Knights Templars, on the plan of The Sepulchre at Jerusalem – that is, with a round body, which becomes octangular above the massive columns, with early and later English additions in the chancel and aisles, and a good later English spire. One of these Templar churches is at Cambridge (lately restored), another at the Temple Gardens, London, though much altered by repairs; and the fourth at Little Maplestead, Essex, which latter is on the model of the Holy Sepulchre, 70 feet long, with a circular body 30 feet in diameter, and timber-roofed.

The town gaol was built in 1846, for 80 prisoners, on the separate system.

Passing up Marefair, is the Grammar School (in Free School Lane), founded in 1556, In what was an old chapel, and rebuilt in 1840. Hervey, who wrote Thern and Aspasia, and the Meditations among the Tombs, was educated here. Further on is a cottage (at the bottom of Black Lyon hill), with an arabesque caning in the lintel; and the west bridge, from which the remains of the castle are seen to the north. This was built by Simon de St Liz, at the Conquest, by the tenure of shoeing the king's horses, and afterwards held by de Montfort and the Barons, against Henry II, who, however, took it by stratagem. It was demolished in 1602, except a round tower, and a house built with the stones, lately occupied by Baker, the county historian. At St Peter's church which was within the precincts, is some Norman work, and a display of grotesque heads and carvings Doddridge's chapel is in this neighbourhood. In College Street, is the Baptist chapel, in which Dr Ryland officiated for 30 years. Bones of an ichthyosaurus have been found in the lias, on the site of St Andrew's priory, in Francis Street. Here also urns have been discovered.

The Infirmary is near the Asylum; a substantial building, founded in 1747. Hereabouts is the new walk, or Victoria Promenade, as it is called, since the Queen passed through in 1844, when a Dispensary was also founded to commemorate that event. The Gothic vault over Becket's well was rebuilt in 1843.

In the neighbourhood are various objects of notice. A series of Saxon and Danish camps on the hills around, as Hunsbury Hill, about 1½ mile from Northampton, in the parish of Hardingstone: in this parish is also Delapre Abbey, the seat of E. Bouverie, Esq., where was an old cluniac house. Rothersthorpe, Castledykes, Clifford Hill, and (further off) Borough Hill, Guilsborough. Close to Delapre Abbey is a Gothic relic, in the shape of Queen Eleanor's Cross, one of the many built by Edward I to the affectionate memory of his excellent wife, at every spot where her body rested on its way to Westminster; it is octangular, in three stories, but was repaired for the worse about a century ago. Here poor Henry VI was defeated and made prisoner by Warwick, 1460, and 'ten thousand tail Englishmen' killed. In Horton Church (near the seat of Sir R. Gunning, Bart.), is an effigy of Queen Catherine Parr's uncle. Courteen Hall, Sir C. Wake, Bart. At Hartwell is a new church. All about Salcey to Pottersbury, Stoney Stratford, Whittlebury, etc., is Crown Forest, which supplied timber for the navy in the war, but is now to be disafforested, on account of its expense. Easton Neston, the Earl of Pomfret's seat, was begun by Wren, and is close to Towcester (eight miles), a small town of shoe and lace makers, which was betrayed to Empson, the avaricious tool of Henry VII. The Talbot Inn is ancient. The Roman Watling Street runs through the town and the hills beyond, which are also traversed by two great modern works – the Grand Junction Canal and the North Western Railway – by means of tunnels at Blisworth and Crick. Fawsley is the fine Tudor seat of Sir C. Knlghtley, Bart., a tory and protectionist of the good old school. Althorp Park (five miles), the sent of Earl Spencer, contains a gallery of pictures, and a library of rare and valuable books, gathered together by the present peer's father, a member of the Roxburghe Club; the family tombs are at Brington. Guilsborough, the seat of W. Ward, Esq., is near a camp on the hills, on the further slope of which, the Avon (Shakspeare's Avon) rises. Overstone (4 miles), belongs to Lord Overstone (formerly S. J. Loyd), the banker, is partly Elizabethan, and partly in the renaissance style, by Inigo Jones. Cottesbrooke, Sir J. Langliam Bart. At Barton Seagrave (seat of Mrs Tibbetts), Sanfoin was first grown by the father of Bridges, the county historian.

Northampton to Market Harborough

A line to Market Harborough here turns off, 18 miles in length. The first station arrived at is Brampton, then

Brixworth, with its good Norman church. The kennels in connection with the celebrated Pytchley Hunt, formerly kept at Pytchley Hall, near Kettering, have been removed here.

Lamport the seat of Sir C. Isham, Bart. Kelmarsh and Clipston stations. At the distance of 3 miles further, we arrive at the small town of

MARKET HARBOROUGH

Population, 2,302. A telegraph station. Hotels – Three Swans; Angel. Market Day – Tuesday. Fairs – Jan. 6th, Feb. 16th, April 29th, July 31st, and Oct. 19th.

This was the place where Charles I fixed his headquarters immediately before the battle of Naseby. The tower is thought to be of Roman origin, having traces of a Roman Camp in the neighbourhood. Its principal trade is in carpets.

Five miles distant is Kibworth Beauchamp, with its rich living of St Wilfrid, value £968, patron, Merton College, Oxon; and its well endowed Free Grammar School, Rev. J. B. Hildebrand, Master. Dr. Aiken was a native, and here Doddridge first preached.

Peterborough Line continued

THE DINING SALOON.
L.& N.W. AMERICAN SPECIAL.

AFTERNOON TEA IN THE SALON-DE-LUXE
L.& N.W. AMERICAN SPECIAL.

COFFEE & CIGARS.
L.& N.W. AMERICAN SPECIAL.

The sumptious interior of carriages on the American Special. This express service commenced in 1898 to take wealthy passengers from Euston direct to Liverpool's Riverside station. This was adjacent to the landing stages for the Cunard and White Star transatlantic liners. The dining saloon is shown at the top, and while the ladies sip their tea the men can relax with their newspapers and cigars. Liverpool Riverside was demolished in the early 1990s. Note the freestanding chairs and furniture – Health and Safety would have a field day. *(CMcC)*

Northampton to Peterborough

Billing Road station.

CASTLE ASHBY

Population, 183. Telegraph station at Wellingbro', 4 miles.
Money Order Office at Wellingbro', 4 miles.

Here is the seat of the Marquis of Northampton, a large quadrangular structure, containing some very rich specimens of oil painting. The dates 1625 and 1635 are seen in the balustrades of the turrets. The castle replaces an old one, having been rebuilt In 1607. Yardley Chase, belonging to it, is 27 miles round. Take notice of the stone parapet hi the court, which is cut so as to make the words, 'Nisi Dominus cedifcaverit domum, in vanum laboraverunt qui cedificant eum.' (Except the Lord build the house, they labour in vain that build it.) Many portraits here. In the park is the church, an elegant building, rendered peculiar from its porch and altar tomb. At Whiston, a good church. At Olney is Cowper's house.

WELLINGBORO'

Population, 6,067. Distance from station, 1 mile. A telegraph station. Hotel – Hind.
Market Day – Wednesday. Fairs – Easter and Whit-Wednesday, and Oct. 29th.

In the neighbourhood of this place are a number of medicinal springs, from which, probably, the name of the town has been given. Charles I and Henrietta, his queen, encamped here a whole season, for the purpose of drinking its waters. It has a very pretty church. Boots, shoes, and lace form its staple trade.

Ditchford station.

HIGHAM FERRERS

Population, 1,152. Distance from station, 1 mile. Telegraph station at Wellingborough, 4½ miles. Hotel – Green Dragon. Market Day – Saturday.
Fairs – Thursday before Feb. 5th, March 7th, May 12th, June 2sth, August 5th, Thursday after August 15th, October 10th, and December 6th.

Boots and shoes are the staple employment here, with lace making. It has a good church, and was the birthplace of Archbishop Chicheley, founder of All Soul's College, Oxford.

Ringstead, Thrapston, Thorpe, and Barnewell stations.

OUNDLE

Population, 2,450. Distance from station, ¾ mile. A telegraph station. Hotel – Talbot.
Market Day – Saturday. Fairs – Feb. 24th, Whit Monday, Aug, 21st, and Oct. 11th.

The town is prettily situated on the banks of the Nene. Dean Park, the seat of the 'last

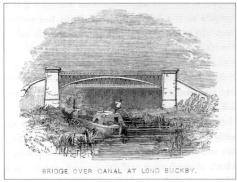

BRIDGE OVER CANAL AT LONG BUCKBY.

Above: The canal bridge at Long Buckby.

Left: The Kilsby Tunnel is rightly heralded as the supreme engineering achievement on the L&BR. Over 7,000 feet long, it features two huge ventilation shafts, one 120 feet deep and the other 60 feet deep. Soon after work had commenced the tunnellers struck an underground quicksand spring, which flooded the works. It took eight months of continuous pumping, day and night, before the tunnel was finished and at a cost of over three times the original estimate.

Left: A Virgin Pendolino tilting on the West Coast Main Line, south of Weedon. *(Cj1340)*

of the Cardigans', and several others, are in its immediate vicinity. Within a distance of three miles is Fotheringay, celebrated in history for its castle, founded by Simon de St Liz, at the Conquest. It was the scene of the nativity of Richard III; and the trial and execution of the ill-fated Mary, Queen of Scots, in 1580. It was demolished by her son. Its situation is indicated by nothing more than a mound of earth.

Elton and Wansford stations.

CASTOR

Population, 745. Distance from station, ¾ mile. Telegraph station at Peterbro', 5 ½ miles. Money Order Office at Peterborough, 4½ miles.

Overton station.

L&NWR Main Line continued

Blisworth to Rugby

Upon leaving this station the line proceeds along an embankment, which terminates after we have crossed the Grand Junction Canal. We then pass the village of Gayton Wharf on the left; thence through a short cutting, we enter a wide extent of beautiful country, called the Valley of the Nene. Occasionally, but only in very clear weather, the town of Northampton can be discerned, about 5 miles distant to the right, and proceeding on along the western declivity of the valley, we pass several villages too numerous to mention. In crossing the Viaduct over the Harstone Brook, we obtain a view of the aqueduct by which the Grand Junction Canal is carried over the stream. Upon issuing from Stonehill tunnel, a short, distance beyond, we are presented with a landscape of unusual beauty, the details of which are frequently shut out from view by the embankment of the canal, but on crossing the Viaduct over the Nene, we obtain a fine prospect of the village of Weedon, and reach the station of that name.

WEEDON

Population, 2,189. A telegraph station. Hotels – Globe, Bull. Omnibuses to Daventry, at 9.22 and 11.25 a.m.; 6 25 p.m. daily.

This village is divided into Upper and Lower Weedon; the latter is bisected by the railway, and the former lies at a short distance on the left. The military depot is a magnificent establishment, and is capable of containing 240,000 stand of small arms. Four miles west of this station is the ancient town of Daventry.

Daventry, near the Nene's Head, and noted for its shoe manufacture, is situated on a gentle eminence near the source of the rivers Avon and Nene. It formerly possessed a rich priory, which Henry VIII gave to Wolsey, the ruins of which are still visible. From Borough Hill, in the vicinity, there is a delightful prospect of Naseby, Northampton, Weedon, and Coventry, and this beautiful landscape is rendered peculiarly picturesque by the remains of a Roman encampment and ramparts in the foreground.

Rugby and rugby

The town centre with the clock tower, dating from 1887, was built to mark Queen Victoria's golden jubilee. The market place is to the left. *(G-Man)*

Left: The stone commemorating William Webb Ellis, who in 1823 ignored the rules of one sport and created another. It is said that one is a game for gentleman played by hooligans, the other a game for hooligans played by gentlemen. The stone is to be found in the school close. *(CMcC)*

Below: London & North Western Railway official postcard showing the Birmingham express at Rugby station, *c.* 1905. *(CMcC)*

From Weedon the line traverses a long cutting, through the occasional openings in which the traveller will catch a glimpse of Brockhall Park and mansion, which has a fine appearance. Proceeding alternately along an embankment, or through a cutting, the most conspicuous object in view is Borough Hill, until we perceive on the right the small village of Watford, and shortly after reach

CRICK
Population, 999. Distance from station, 3 miles. Telegraph station at Rugby, 65 miles. Money Order Office at Weedon, 5½ miles.

The village of Crick lies to the north of the station, and is a place of no importance. The canal passes under a tunnel here 1,524 yards in length, through the hills which stretch before us, and which is the boundary between the counties of Northampton and Warwick. They form also the separating ridge between the valley of the Avon, and that of the Ouse and Nene, and contain the sources of rivers which flow to different sides of the island. In approaching them, we enter a cutting which gradually becomes deeper and deeper, and at length brings us to the Grand Kilsby Tunnel, on emerging from which we perceive a wooded but uninteresting country, the entrance to

WARWICKSHIRE

The general aspect of which is an agreeable alternation of hill and dale, exceedingly well suited for agricultural purposes. The insulated situation of the county, and its freedom from great inequalities of surface, render the climate mild, and vegetation early. As the train proceeds further into the county, the scenery assumes a more pleasing character. Several villages are spread over the hills on the right, among which is Brownsover, the birth place of Lawrence Sheriff, founder of Rugby School, and shortly after we arrive at

RUGBY
Population, 7,818. A telegraph station. Hotels – Royal, and Eagle. Market Day – Saturday. Fairs – Feb. 17th, March 31st, May 15th, July 7th; Aug. 21st, Monday before 29th Sept., Nov. 22nd, and Dec. 10th. Bankers – National Provincial Bank of England; Butlins & Sons.

From Rugby several lines of railway, as the Trent Valley, Midland, Leamington, &c., branch off, making it a sort of starting point in the centre of England. It was this convenient position which made the late Sir R. Peel, at the opening of the Trent Valley Railway, propose Rugby as a good point to which the general office should be transferred. There is here a Deaf and Dumb College, lately founded, with an old Gothic church, restored by Richman, whose Essay on the subject contributed so much to the revival of this picturesque church style. Rugby stands near the river Avon, on a slight elevation (called Rocheberie at the Conquest) above the lias plain, between Watling Street and Dunsmore Heath. This healthy spot was fixed on by Lawrence Sheriff, a

Top: The Pump Room in Leamington Spa which, Bradshaw tells us, 'fifty years since, was an obscure and humble village, is now, though still rural and picturesque, become a large and handsome town.'

Middle left: The Regent Hotel in Leamington. *(Cornell University Library)*

Left: The 'magnificent ruins' of Kenilworth Castle. *(Cornell University Library)*

London tradesman, but a native of Brownsover, close by, for his school, which was founded in 1507, and endowed with property now worth nearly £7,000 a year. By the exertions of successive masters, especially the late Dr Arnold, it ranks as one of the best grammar schools in the country. There are about a dozen masters, for whom, by a liberal arrangement, retiring pensions are provided; and 60 foundation scholars; besides 200 who pay, and who really give the tone to the institution. The School was rebuilt in the Tudor style in 1808, by Hakewell, with a front of 220 feet long; prize compositions are recited in the great room on Easter Wednesday. In the chapel are monuments to Doctors James and Arnold, the former by Chantrey. One of the prizes was established in honour of Dr Arnold's memory, by the Queen, after the appearance of Stanley's most useful and interesting life of him. He was born at Cowes, and died here almost suddenly on June 12th, 1842. The fagging or monitor system prevails, as at most other large schools, but it was somewhat mitigated by the influence of Dr Arnold. Parkhurst Cave, Gent, Abercromby Bray, the antiquary, Dr Butler (the admirable Master of Shrewsbury School), and Sir H. Halford were educated here.

Some old gable houses remain at Rugby. Fossils are occasionally dug in the blue lias. The castle on the east side occupies the site of a Norman castle, which was dismantled by Henry II.

Within a short distance are the following: Coton Hall (4 miles), the Hon. C. L. Butler's seat, has a good prospect; Newnham Paddox (5 miles), the ancient seat of the Earl of Denbigh, close to Watling Street, which here runs along the county border. Ashby St Ledger's, Lady Senbourne's seat, was formerly that of the Catesby family, one of whom was Robert Catesby, who shared in the Gunpowder Plot. The church is ancient. To the west of Rugby are, Holbrook Grange, seat of J. Caldecott, Esq. Coombe Abbey and Coventry are further off. Danes Moor or Dunsmoor Heath was the appointed rendezvous of Catesby and his fellow plotters. At Stretton (where a Roman road or street is crossed) was a reformatory school for young criminals, established in 1817, but since given up from want of support.

Rugby and Leamington branch

Rugby to Leamington and Warwick

Without stopping at the stations of Birdingbury and Marton, we pass on to

LEAMINGTON

LN&WR, the Avenue station, centrally situated, and Great Western.
A telegraph station. Hotels – The Regent, Clarendon, and Bath.
Bankers – Leamington Priors & Warwickshire Banking Company; Warwick & Leamington Banking Company. Races in March, September, and November.

Leamington Spa, which fifty years since was an obscure and humble village, is now, though still rural and picturesque, become a large and handsome town, containing 17,958 inhabitants, and is proverbial for being better paved, lighted, and regulated, than

LMS locos
Above: No. 6100, *Royal Scot* of the Royal Scot class. Built in 1927 by the North British Locomotive Company, it is one of two preserved examples of this class. *Left:* LMS No. 6207, *Princess Arthur of Connaught* of the Princess Royal class. *Below:* No. 6166 *London Rifle Brigade,* another Scot. *(CMcC)*

any other town of its size in the kingdom. The Hotels are princely, both as to size and comfort; and the Shops equal to those in the metropolis. It abounds also with elegant houses and detached villas, and the lodging houses for visitors are most convenient and well-arranged. Its extraordinary rise and present importance is attributable to its Celebrated Water and Baths, the curative properties of which are so fully established as to be annually resorted to by vast numbers of invalids, besides a constant succession of fashionable visitors. Leamington possesses, among its numerous attractions, a splendid Tennis Court and Racket Ground, attached to an elegant pile of buildings, forming the Club Rooms of the leading members of the Aristocracy of Warwickshire. It has two Newspapers, the Advertiser and the Courier, the former published on Thursday, and the latter on Saturday; a Literary and Scientific Institution, Public Libraries and News Rooms, on an unusually spirited scale. Assembly Rooms, Music Hall, Theatre Royal, Pump Rooms and Baths; and for the admirers of the noble game of Cricket, a ground kept by the two acknowledged best players in England. Both at Leamington and in the neighbourhood, the fashionable sport of Archery is much practised, there being clubs at Leamington and Wellesboume, in addition to that connected with the renowned Forest of Arden.

Leamington is remarkable for its salubrity; is situated in the midst of a finely wooded and romantic neighbourhood, is contiguous to Warwick Castle, the fine old town of Warwick, the magnificent ruins of Kenilworth Castle, the beautiful Park of Stoneleigh Abbey, Guy's Cliff, Offchurch Bury; the interesting town of Stratford-upon-Avon, renowned as the birth-place of the immortal Shakespeare; the City of Coventry, full of antiquities: and Birmingham, celebrated for its arts and manufactures. Coombe Abbey, Wroxhall Abbey, Compton Verney, Compton Wynyates; Edge hill, the scene of the great battle during the reign of Charles I; Charlecote; Hampton Lucy; The Jephson Gardens, delightfully situated in the centre of Leamington, are easily accessible to visitors, and very attractive. During the summer season a first-rate band performs there daily; and Galas, Archery, and Horticultural Fetes are frequently held in them.

The 'Arboretum and Pinetum' established by John Hitchman, Esq., comprises upwards of eleven acres, formed for the exclusive cultivation and sale of plants, contains an extensive collection of Deciduous and choice Coniferous Trees and Rare Shrubs, Roses, Rhododendrons, etc. The far-famed Warwickshire Hounds hunt within an easy distance of the Spa, rendering the winter season at Leamington particularly gay. The Hunting Season commences about the middle of October, and the Warwickshire country is now hunted daily by the North and South Warwickshire Packs. A pack of Hounds is kept at the Leamington Kennels; and other arrangements are made particularly advantageous to gentlemen for this enjoyment. The Leamington College is established upon the principle of our public foundation schools, for the education of the sons of Noblemen and Gentlemen, and under the superintendence of distinguished masters. The railway communication by the Great Western and North Western Companies, each of which has a station in the town, brings Leamington within reach of visitors from every part of the kingdom; and it will be found on investigation, that whether for a permanent residence or for occasional resort, few places possess so many attractions as this highly favoured town.

Warwick Castle

Warwick and its immediate neighbour, Leamington, were on a branch from Rugby. Bradshaw dismises Warwick as 'a dull town', although he does admire the castle. Since 1978 it has been owned by the Tussauds Group and is now a major tourist destination.

Left: The Castle's Grand Hall. *(Cornell University Library) Below:* Photocrom view of the castle walls, *c.* 1895. *(LoC)*

Right: West Gate and the chapel of St James, built by the 12th Earl of Warwick, Robert Beauchamp. The building to the right of the photograph is the Lord Leycester Hospital in Warwick, a retirement home for disabled ex-servicemen. *(National Media Museum)*

WARWICK

Population, 10,570. A telegraph station. Hotels – Warwick Arms, Mrs Lake, family hotel and posting house. Woolpack, John Court, family and commercial, very good

Market Day – Saturday. Fairs – 3rd Monday in Jan., 2nd Monday in Feb., Monday before April 5th, 1st Saturday in Lent, 1st Monday in June, 2nd Monday in Aug., Monday before St Thomas, May 12th, July 5th, Sept. 4th, Oct. 12th, Nov. 8th, and Dec. 21st. Mails – Two arrivals and departures, daily, between London and Warwick.

Money Order Office. Bankers – Messrs. Greenway & Greaves; Leamington-Priors & Warwickshire Company; Warwick & Leamington Banking Company.

Warwick is a dull town, in the county of Warwick. The Castle is one of the finest specimens in the kingdom of the ancient residences of our feudal ancestors. Its appearance, overhanging the Avon, and surrounded by majestic masses of trees, is extremely picturesque, and the views from its lofty turrets are magnificent.

Passing through a road cut through the solid rock, which now presents a plantation of shrubs judiciously arranged, so as to shut out the view of this noble pile till it is suddenly presented to the eye, the visitor finds himself in a spacious area, where he is at once surrounded by ancient fortifications, and Gothic buildings of a later date, now devoted to more peaceful occupations than those of the old chieftains. The keep is no more than a picturesque ruin, hut two towers of great antiquity are still entire.

From Guy's Tower the views are exceedingly fine. On the north side lies the town, of which you have a beautiful bird's-eye view. Far stretching in the distance are seen the spires of Coventry churches; the castle of Kenilworth; Guy's Cliff and Blacklow Hill; Grove Park; Shuckburgh and Shropshire Hills; the Saxon Tower on the Broadway Hill; the fashionable Spa of Leamington, which appears almost lying at your feet; while village churches lifting up their venerable heads from amidst embosoming trees, fill up a grand and interesting picture. A fine collection of pictures – splendid staterooms – fitted up in accordance with the general style of the building, and an extensive armoury, lend a gorgeous air of completeness to this princely and magnificent establishment.

The castellated remains of old England are all of them 'beautiful for situation'; but few comprise so many objects of natural and historic interest as Warwick Castle. Standing at the windows of the great hall, the prospect which meets the eye is most delightful.

The spacious and elegant conservatory contains the famous Warwick Vase, which was dug up from the ruins of the Emperor Adrian's Villa at Tivoli. It is considered one of the most entire, and to a certain extent, one of the most beautiful specimens of ancient sculpture which this country possesses. The material of which it is made is white marble. Its form is nearly spherical, with a deep reverted rim. Two interlacing vines, whose stems twine into and constitute the handles, wreath their tendrils with fruit and foliage round the upper part. The centre is composed of antique heads which stand forward In grand relief. A panther's skin, with the thyrsus of Bacchus (a favourite antique ornament), and other embellishments complete the composition. The size of this vase is immense, and it is capable of containing a hundred and sixty-three gallons.

Above: The 'noble' viaduct across the River Avon, between Rugby and Coventry.

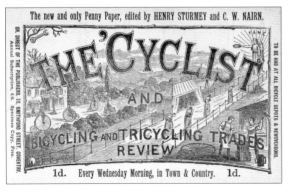

The transport museum in Coventry has a gallery devoted to the many local bicycle manufacturers. The city was a centre for both bicycle and motor cycle makers and this led directly to the growth of the motor industry in the Midlands.

Above left: Mr Doyle poses with his 'ordinary', made by the Coventry Machinists Company in 1873. *(NLI)*

Left: The Cyclist, 'The new and only Penny Paper', published in Coventry.

Rugby to Birmingham and Stafford

Upon leaving the station the line proceeds along an embankment which affords a very pleasing prospect of the valley on the right, in which the Swift and several other small rivers unite their waters to form the Avon. Newbold-upon-Avon appears prettily situated on the opposite side of the valley, and across the fields on the left is Baton, where Addison spent the evening of his life.

Five miles from Rugby the line reaches the Brandon embankment which is two miles in length, and affords some beautiful prospects.

It then crosses the Avon by a noble viaduct, and for a time the river gives a highly picturesque character to the scenery on the left.

After passing through a cutting we enter a wide extent of open country, and catch the first glimpse of the magnificent Coventry spires. From the embankment along which we proceed we can also see on the right, Stoke, Ernsford, Grange, Bromley, and the woods surrounding Coombe Abbey. The line crosses the Sowe by a beautiful viaduct of seven arches, and soon after the spires of Coventry rise distinctly above the intervening woods. We pass Whitley Abbey, which stands conspicuously on the left, cross a seven-arched viaduct over the Sherbourne Valley, enter a deep cutting, and shortly after we reach the station at

COVENTRY

A telegraph station. Hotel – King's Head. Market Day – Friday. Fairs – 2nd Friday after Ash Wednesday, May 2nd, Friday in Trinity week, Aug. 26th add 27th, and Nov. 1st. Bankers – Warwickshire Banking Co.; Coventry Union Banking Co.; Messrs. Little & Woodcock; Coventry & Warwick Banking Co.

The fine steeples of St Michael's and Trinity are the first to strike one in this old city, which is the seat of the ribbon trade, and a parliamentary borough, 94 miles from London. It returns two members, and has a population of 41,647. Woollens and blue thread were formerly the staple manufactures; but they are now superseded by ribbons and watches, two branches introduced by the French refugees of the 17th century. About 2,000 hands are employed on the latter, and upwards of 30,000 on silk weaving, throwing, and the weaving and dyeing of ribbons. Alabar and power looms are chiefly used in the manufacture. This trade in late years has greatly increased; many steam factories having been erected: one just completed for Mr Hart is capable of holding about 300 large looms, and will give employment to 1,000 hauds, producing as many ribbons as the whole town could make in 1830. Many women and children are employed French ribbons ore imported by the dealers; but in point of taste as well as cheapness, English productions are now a fair rival to foreign ones. Coventry (like Covent Garden in London) takes its name from a monastery, founded in the 11th century, by Leofric, the Saxon, and his wife Godiva, whose memory is honoured by an occasional procession. According to the well known story, she obtained a grant of privileges to the town by

Above left: A statue of the eleventh-century celebrity Lady Godiva by John Thomas. Not doing a very good job of maintaining her modesty. *(Linda Spashett Storye_book) Above right:* A special service held for soldiers in 1945 within the ruins of Coventry Cathedral. Compare this with the same view at the top of the opposite page. *(CMcC)*

Below: The Whittle Arch, built to commemorate the Coventry-born jet engine pioneer Sir Frank Whittle. It is located in front of the excellent Coventry Transport Museum. *(G-Man)*

Three panoramic photographs of Coventry city centre taken from the cathedral tower in August 2011. *(Si mintchocicecream)*

consenting to ride naked through the streets. To save her delicacy, the people closed their windows and abstained from looking, except Peeping Tom, whose bust, adorned with a pigtail, stands at the corner of Hertford Street. Many old fashioned gable houses are to be seen here in the narrow back streets. The Guildhall is a fine middle-age building, with a timbered hall, adorned with escutcheons and stained windows. Another old pile, is the House of Industry, near some remains of a priory. Three gates, and fragments of the town walls, the Free Grammar School, Bablake's old hospital (1330), the church, and the Exchange, a handsome building containing a noble hall, recently erected from designs by Mr James Murray, deserve notice. The beautiful steeple of St Michael's on the Gothic church, is about 300 feet high; it was built by the two Botoners, mayors of the town, between 1373 and '95; near it stands part of a palace belonging to the bishops, when Coventry was a diocese with Lichfield. The Cathedral, dissolved by Henry VIII, stood at Hill Close. Trinity, or the priory church is also Gothic, with a steeple 237 feet high, of later date. Here the Grey Friars acted their miracle plays at the feast of Corpus Christi – a series of Bible dramas, from the Creation to Doomsday. Henry VI often came to see them. Coventry has an important School of Design.

Within a distance of two miles are Whitley Park, an old Elizabethan seat of Viscount Hood. Kenilworth Castle (6 miles), the road to which is along an avenue of noble trees, the Gale Home at which should be visited, on account of the large sculptured mantel piece in it. Dr Butler Was a native. Stoneleigh, Park, Lord Leigh, with some Abbey ruins, a portrait of Byron,, and Zaffary's famous one, 'Garrick telling a Ghost story', Packington, Earl of Aylesford; Coombe Abbey, Earl Craven, has Abbey ruins, with a gallery of Vandykes, Lelys, etc., and remains of an Abbey at Berkswell, seat of Sir J. Wilmot, Bart., at which is Canaletti's view of London.

Coventry to Birmingham

On leaving Coventry the line passes through several cuttings, in the openings of which a fine view may be obtained of the city, with its lofty spires, rising majestically from the dense mass of houses. The line continues through several cuttings, which exclude nearly all view of the country.

Allesley Gate station.

BERKSWELL

Population, 1,624. Distance from station, 1 mile.

Telegraph station at Coventry, 5½ miles. Money Order Office at Coventry, 5½ miles.

The landscape improves somewhat here, and we have views of several line seats, comprising Mercote Hall, Packington Park, and Berkswell Hall, Sir J. Wilmot, Bart. After crossing the Blythe, by a viaduct of noble proportions, the traveller will perceive on the left, a very old, and almost ruined bridge, with five arches, which, with a quaint windmill and rich surrounding country, form a pretty picture.

HAMPTON (Junction)

Population, 690. Distance from station, ¾ mile. Telegraph station at Whitacre, 7¼ miles.

Hotel – Railway. Money Order Office at Coleshill, 4½ miles.

The village of Hampton lies on the left of the line, and consists of little to interest the traveller. Two miles beyond is Elmdon Hall.

MARSTON GREEN

Distance from station, ¾ mile. Telegraph station at Birmingham, 6½ miles.

Money Order Office at Coleshill, 4 miles.

After passing under Marston Hall bridge we traverse some prettily wooded country, having Marston Wood on the right, and Elmdon Park on the left. On reaching the Sheldon embankment, a prospect is obtained which is considered equal in beauty to any which the line affords. On the right is Alcot Park, the town and church of Coleshill, and Maxtoke Park on the left. Elmdon, with its fine woodlands, and the pretty village of Sheldon; whilst in advance, the high spire of Yardley church completes the landscape. A short cutting brings us opposite the village of Yardley, near enough to admire the fine tower and spire of the church.

STECHFORD

Distance from station, ½ mile. Telegraph station at Birmingham, 3¾ miles.

Money Order Office at Coleshill, 6 miles.

Shortly after leaving this station, we obtain an imperfect glimpse of Birmingham, which soon extends into a full and splendid view. From the vast and dense mass of confused buildings rise the beautiful spires of its several churches, and the tall chimnies of its still more numerous manufactories; whilst proudly conspicuous in the centre, the Town Hall lifts its noble front.

Barr Beacon is visible on the right, with Aston church, park, and hall. Ashted and Vauxhall soon afterwards appear, and not far distant the Grand Junction Railway is seen stretching away in a northerly direction.

Curzon Street station

The original Birmingham terminus for the L&BR was Curzon Street. Opened in 1838 as Birmingham station, it also served the Grand Junction Railway with the two companies having adjacent platforms. As with Euston, the entrance building with its imposing columns was designed by Philip Hardwick. The railway companies merged in 1846 and from 1854 they shared the New Street station with the Midland Railway. Although passenger services ceased from Curzon Street, some special excursion trains continued to use the station until 1893, and it continued as a goods station until closure in 1966.

Unlike Euston, the Curzon Street station building has survived intact. The side arches in J. C. Bourne's engraving of the station, shown at the top, were never built. The coat of arms for both London and Birmingham are represented in the large decorative relief above the front door. The commemorative plaque is to the right of the great doors. *(Peter James)*

Birmingham

Telegraph stations – Temple Buildings, New Street, and the railway stations.
Hotels – The Queen's, North Western Central Railway Station, New Street, first-class hotel, for families and gentlemen. Dee's Royal; The Stork; King's Head; Nelson and Swan. Omnibuses to and from the station.
Market Days – Monday, Thursday, and Saturday. Fairs – Whit-Thursday, and Thursday nearest September 29th. Bankers – Attwood & Co.; Moilliet & Co.; Taylors & Lloyds; Birmingham Banking Co.; Birmingham & Midland Banking Co.; Branch Bank of England; National Provincial Bank of England; Town & District Banking Co.

This is the great centre of the manufactured metal trades, being situated in North Warwickshire, on the border of the South Staffordshire iron and coal district – 112 miles from London by the North Western railway, or 129 miles by the Great Western Railway. The town stands upon a series of sandstone hills, of moderate elevation; it is well-drained, and very healthy, although containing a population of 296,076 inhabitants.

Steam power is here used extensively, scarcely a street being without its manufactory and steam engine; at same time a considerable amount of the labour is of a manual kind, carried on in small workshops attached to the dwelling-houses of the artisans; and, it is worthy of remark, that the houses of the poorer classes here are very superior to those usually met with in large manufacturing or densely inhabited towns.

The public buildings most worthy of note in Birmingham are – first the Town Hall, at the top of New Street, a beautiful Grecian Temple, of Mona marble, 166 feet by 100, on a basement 23 feet high, surrounded by rows of Corinthian pillars, 40 feet high; it has a splendid public hall, 145 feet long, at one end of which is the famous organ by Hill, one of the finest in Europe, containing 4,000 pipes, acted upon by four sets of keys. In this hall is held the celebrated Triennial Musical Festival, perhaps the most successful of anything of the kind, drawing together talented artistes from all parts of the world to aid in the performances; here also is a fine bust of Mendelssohn, who presided in this Hall in 1846, at the first performance of his *Elijah*. The Market Hall is a fine building of stone, 365 feet long, 103 feet wide, and 60 high, with 600 stalls. It is situated in High Street. King Edward the Sixth's Grammar School, in New Street, founded in 1522, and endowed with twenty pounds' worth of land by the monarch whose name it bears, was rebuilt by Barry, in the Gothic style, with a frontage of 174 feet long and 60 feet high. Its income is now about £11,000 a-year, arising principally from the increased value of its lands. The Queen's College, in Paradise Street, founded by Mr Sands Cox, in 1843, and built in the Tudor style, has various professorships attached to it, some of them endowed by that liberal contributor, Dr Warneford. In Summer Lane is the General Hospital a noble institution, founded in 1760, by Dr Ash. The celebrated musical festivals already mentioned are held for the benefit of this establishment. The Queen's Hospital, in Bath Row, the Deaf and Dumb Asylum, the Blind Asylum, Lying-in-Hospital, Infirmary,

Bradshaw describes many of the manufacturers in Birmingham. *Above left:* Manufactory & Show Rooms in New Street. *Above:* Promotional card for Joe Wragg's Super Quality Soda. *(CMcC)*

The civic face of the city. *Left:* The Town Hall with illuminations for the coronation of George VI in 1937. *(CMcC) Below:* Birmingham's Council House. *(G-Man)*

Magdalen Asylum, Ragged and Industrial Schools, and a Reformatory, have all more or less handsome and suitable buildings. The Blue Coat School is an excellent institution, with an extensive stone building, where are maintained and educated 200 boys and girls; it is situated in St Philip's churchyard, and is entirely supported by voluntary contributions. Bingley Hall is an immense sited, covering nearly two acres of ground, where the Midland Cattle and Poultry Shows are held in December of every year, and which have now become the most extensive and successful in the country. The Gaol, Lunatic Asylum, and the Workhouse. The Birmingham and Midland Institute, in course of erection, adjoining the Town Hall, will be a noble pile of building; the foundation stone was laid by H.R.H. Prince Albert, in November, 1855. Opposite the Town Hall is a colossal statue in bronze, of the late Sir Robert Peel, by Peter Hollins; and opposite the Market Hall, another of Nelson, by Westmacott.

Edgbaston, the 'West End' of Birmingham, where the wealthy manufacturers live, is a beautifully arranged collection of villa residences.

The parish church is St Martin's, in the Bull Ring, originally built in the thirteenth century, and having tombs of the De Berminghams, who founded a castle here in 1155. Some of the oldest houses are in this, quarter; in front is Westmacott's statue of Nelson, on a column. St George's Church is a Gothic structure, built in 1822 by Packman. St Paul's is marked by a good spire. St Philip's, in the upper part of the town, has a large churchyard. Christ Church, St Mary's, St Bartholomew's, Trinity, St Thomas's, St James's, St Peter's, All Saints' and about twelve more of recent erection. There is a Roman Catholic cathedral, in brick, by Pugin. The Jews have a splendid Synagogue, lately erected at Singers' Hill.

The principal Establishments worth visiting in Birmingham are:

Electro-Plate and Sliver. The establishment of Messrs. Elkington, Mason, & Co., in Newhall Street, perhaps without an equal in the world, taking into consideration its range of beautiful show rooms, in connection with its workshops, where may be seen the manufacturing of silver goods, electro-plated wares, and bronzes, in every possible stage.

Steel Pen Manufacturer. We should think the reputation of Messrs. Gillott & Son, Graham Street, has reached all parts of the world.

From Birmingham many interesting excursions may be made within a circle of about 20 miles. Among these are Kenilworth and Warwick Castles; Stratford-on-Avon, the birth-place of Shakespeare near Charlecote, the Lucy's seat; Tamworth Castle, near Drayton Manor, the seat of Sir R. Peel; Lichfield Cathedral and town, where Dr Johnson was born; the iron and coal fields to the north, round Wednesbury, Walsall, Bilston, and other seats of the hardware trade, all honeycombed below, intersected by canals and railways above; Sandwell Park, Earl Dartmouth's seat, and Oscott Roman Catholic College; Dudley Castle and caves; Leasowes (which was Shenstone's seat), and Hagley Park, near Hales Owen; the fine country round Kidderminster and Stourport, on the Severn.

Above: The Lucas works in Birmingham, dressed up for the coronation in 1937. *(CMcC)* *Left:* Bull at the entrance to the Bullring. *(Luke Byfield)* *Bottom left:* The Library of Birmingham in Centenary Square. *(Elliott Brown) Below:* The BT Tower, built 1965. *(Erebus555)*

The Central Station. The progressive extension of the railway system led to the erection of several buildings for its general purposes; and these structures are entitled to rank amongst toe- most stupendous architectural works of the age.

It was built for the accommodation of the immense traffic of the London and North Western, and that of the Midland, Stour Valley, and South Staffordshire lines.

Situated in New Street, Birmingham, the entrance is at the bottom of Stephenson Place, through an arcade, to the booking offices for the respective railways; passing through these we emerge on a magnificent corridor or gallery, guarded by a light railing, and open to the station (but enclosed by the immense glass and iron roof), from whence broad stone staircases, with bronze rails, afford access to the departure platform. We then stand on a level' with a long series of offices, appropriated to the officials of the company, and a superb refreshment room, divided into three portions by rows of massive pillars, annexed to which is an hotel (the Queen's).

The interior of this station deserves attention from its magnitude. The semicircular roof is 1,100 feet long, 205 feet wide, and 80 feet high, composed of iron and glass, without the slightest support except that afforded by the pillars on either side. If the reader notice the turmoil and bustle created by the excitement of the arrival and departure of trains, the trampling of crowds of passengers, the transport of luggage, the ringing of bells, and the noise of two or three hundred porters and workmen, he will retain a recollection of the extraordinary scene witnessed daily at the Birmingham Central Railway Station.

Below: Queens & North Western Hotel, adjoining New Street station. LNWR postcard. (*CMcC*)

A female member of British Railways staff transports packages and parcels on a Greenwood & Bately battery-powered truck at Euston station in the days before the great rebuild.

Acknowledgements
Thanks go the following sources for providing additional images for this book: Campbell McCutcheon *(CMcC)*, US Library of Congress *(LoC)*, Johnny Greig, Man Vyi, Hugh Llewelyn, Cnbrb, Tom Walker, Michael Jamieson, Martin Pettitt, Ted Coles, Central Intelligence Agency *(CIA)*, Ted Coles, Viki Male, Simon, Cj1340, David Merrett, G-Man, Tony Hisgett, Cornell University Library, National Media Museum, National Library of Ireland *(NLI)*, Si mintchocicecream, Peter James, Elliott Brown, Luke Byfield and Erebus555. Unless otherwise stated, new photography is by John and Jay Christopher.